THE

BAFFLED PARENT'S

GUIDE TO

Coaching Indoor Youth

SOCCER

Also by Ned McIntosh

Little League® Drills and Strategies

The Little League® Guide to Tee Ball

Managing Little League® Baseball

THE BAFFLED PARENT'S
GUIDE TO
COACHING INDOOR YOUTH
SOCCER

Ned McIntosh
Jeff Thaler

Ragged Mountain Press/McGraw-Hill

Camden, Maine • New York • San Francisco • Washington, D.C. • Auckland
Bogotá • Caracas • Lisbon • London • Madrid • Mexico City • Milan • Montreal
New Delhi • San Juan • Singapore • Sydney • Tokyo • Toronto

Official rules and referee signals (Chapter 10) are excerpted from *The Official Rules of Indoor Soccer*, Youth and Amateur Edition, © United States Indoor Soccer Association, 2003. Reprinted with permission.

Material from *Indoor Soccer* reprinted with permission of Sterling Publishing Co., Inc., © 1995 by Evert Tuenissen. English translation © 1997 by Sterling Publishing Co., Inc. Originally published by BV Uitgeversmaatschappi Tirion, under the title *Zaal Voetbal*.

1 2 3 4 5 6 7 8 9 0 DOC/DOC 2 1 0 9 8 7 6 5 4 3

ISBN 0-07-141143-7

Photographs on pages 7, 8, and 16 courtesy of Street Soccer Cup USA
All other interior photographs by David Orbock, t/a Village Gallery, Towson, MD, and George Leukel, Ocean City, MD
Diagrams by Robert F. Hagan, Chesapeake Promotional Services

McGraw-Hill books are available at special quantity discounts to use as premiums and sales promotions, or for use in corporate training programs. For more information, please write to the Director of Special Sales, Professional Publishing, McGraw-Hill, Two Penn Plaza, New York, NY 10121-2298. Or contact your local bookstore.

This book is printed on acid-free paper.

We dedicate this book to our wives, Rina Thaler and Elaine McIntosh, and the kids who play indoor soccer at the Ocean City, Maryland, Recreation Complex, pictured in this book—especially those close to us, whose pictures are shown here.

From left: rear row, coauthors Ned McIntosh and Jeff. M. Thaler; front row, Parker McIntosh, Duncan McIntosh, Brandon Thaler, and Chelsea Thaler

Contents

Chapter 12: Winning   107

Introduction

This book is the latest in the highly successful McGraw-Hill series of Baffled Parents guides. Coauthor Ned McIntosh discovered what it is to be a baffled parent when he took his nine-year-old son, Tommy, to register for an AYSO outdoor soccer league in Chatsworth, California. He was told there were more children registered than coaches to handle them, and the only way Tommy could be assured of being assigned to a team would be if his dad would volunteer to coach his son's team. "But I've never played soccer," he protested. "No problem," he was told. "We'll give you a rule book and a high school player to assist you." With the word "please!" forming on his son's lips, what choice did Ned have? He wondered how many other coaches were recruited the same way. But he remembered that recruiting ploy later when *he* had to recruit parent/coaches to help him.

As the successful author of three prior books on youth sports, Ned McIntosh knew the formula for writing them: find a new sport that is growing in popularity, then write the first book about it. It worked for him when he wrote the first published book on Little League baseball in 1985. Entitled *Managing Little League Baseball*, it has sold more than 100,000 copies to date. Its sales continue at a high level annually because more new children join the ranks of Little League each year, along with a new group of baffled parent/coaches looking for a how-to book to help them coach.

Now a grandfather, McIntosh was first introduced to *indoor* soccer when his two grandsons invited him to watch their games. Clearly intrigued by what one coach calls "pinball soccer," with constant action in high-scoring games, McIntosh wanted to learn more about the game. He wanted to help his grandsons, who were very enthusiastic about the sport, but he recognized that his experience coaching outdoor soccer would not be enough, as the indoor game was significantly different. Looking for a how-to book on coaching indoor soccer, he went through a period of frustrating research just as he had done 17 years earlier when he'd sought a book on coaching Little League baseball. He searched bookstores, the library, and the Internet for an appropriate book. His Internet research convinced him that there is a burgeoning interest in the sport—with more than three million children playing it—but no books to help a baffled grandparent learn how to coach it.

To find confirmation about the general popularity of youth soccer, and indoor youth soccer in particular, he obtained a national survey conducted by the Soccer Industry Council of America in the year 2000, "United States Soccer Market" (Exhibit I.1). It reported that nearly 14 million U.S. boys and girls in the age range six through seventeen are playing soccer; more than half of them are between the ages of six and twelve.

But how many of those 14 million youngsters are playing *indoor* soccer? McIntosh started his research on the Internet, and 30,000 websites appeared when the phrase *indoor youth soccer* was used as the keywords. Further research among the leading national organizations that sponsor indoor youth soccer provided interpolated data that at least three million youngsters between the ages of eight and eighteen are playing indoor soccer in the United States. That appeared to be a conservative estimate, as it is only 21 percent of the 14 million youngsters who play soccer, according to the Soccer Industry survey. Ironically, however, three million is approximately the same number of youngsters that were playing Little League baseball when McIntosh's groundbreaking book on that sport was first published

Age	Number of Male Participants	Number of Female Participants	Total
6–11	4,701,000	3,166,000	7,867,000
12–17	2,924,000	3,042,000	5,966,000
18–24	1,108,000	629,000	1,737,000
25–34	1,057,000	275,000	1,332,000
35+	889,000	387,000	1,276,000
Totals	10,679,000	7,499,000	18,178,000

- Soccer participation is booming among males and females.

- 76 percent (14 million) of all participants are under 18.

- Soccer is America's number one family sport.

- Median soccer household income is $58,000.

- Soccer players in the United States actively participate in other youth-oriented sports: basketball, baseball, fast-pitch softball.

EXHIBIT I.1   Survey showing popularity of youth soccer in the United States Source: 2000 Soccer Industry Council of America

in 1985. So both criteria had been met to justify a book: a new sport growing in popularity, with no published book to help baffled parent/coaches. That was enough evidence to convince him, and for him to convince McGraw-Hill, that a book on coaching indoor youth soccer was needed.

The only problem McIntosh faced in writing a book on *indoor* youth soccer was his lack of experience with the indoor game. His experience coaching *outdoor* soccer was not enough background when contrasted with his writing on Little League baseball, where he'd had 20 years' experience coaching his three sons. Therefore, he concluded that he should look for a coauthor with significant experience in coaching the sport. It had to be a coach who endorsed McIntosh's philosophy of "Keep it simple and make it fun." He was concerned about the growing incidence of parents and/or coaches taking the fun out of youth sports through an overemphasis on winning.

Unfortunately in Little League baseball, during the past 17 years, the so-called Little League rage problem among parents and coaches had reached epidemic proportions nationwide, which was taking the fun out of playing for many of the youngsters. McIntosh was determined to find, in addition to a good indoor youth soccer coach, one whose experience was in the most positive environment possible. He solved the problem by contacting the administrator of the indoor soccer league in which his 11-year-old grandson, Parker, participates. This league plays its games in the modern two-arena complex at the Ocean City, Maryland, Recreation Complex. The league is affiliated with NAYS (National Alliance of Youth Sports), an organization McIntosh knew and respected. It trains and certifies its volunteer coaches, and embraces the same child-friendly philosophy that McIntosh espoused in his three books on youth sports. He told Wendy Bills, administrator of the indoor soccer league, what he had in mind and asked if she could recommend a volunteer coach, one who epitomized the high standards of NAYS, to serve as his coauthor. She suggested Jeff Thaler, coach of an indoor soccer team that included his 10-year-old twins, Brandon and Chelsea. Jeff played soccer at the collegiate level and has a strong background as a volunteer parent/coach of both outdoor and indoor soccer teams. He also is an experienced coach of Little League baseball, which gave him a common coaching background with McIntosh. The fact that Thaler's twins are a boy and a girl was a bonus as well, since youth soccer attracts more girls as participants than Little League baseball does, and some of the girls, particularly in the 12-and-under age-groups, are excellent players.

At a time when interest in girls soccer has grown in popularity nationally, including at the Olympic and World Cup levels, McIntosh concluded that even more baffled parent/coaches of daughters as well as sons could benefit from a how-to book on coaching indoor youth soccer.

The two players in this indoor soccer scrimmage illustrate the popularity of the sport among girls, especially in the U12 and younger teams.

One last potential problem faced the two coauthors. Both were convinced, based on their coaching experience, that there is a direct correlation between practice and playing well; i.e., the more a youngster practices the basic skills of the game, the better he or she plays, and the better he or she plays, the more fun the game will be. That may sound like obvious conclusions, but it also translated into a team phenomenon: the more a team practiced, the more games it won. The team whose coach never held practice between games had a losing season; the team whose coach maximized the opportunities for practice had a winning season. Clearly, winning is more fun than losing, and the team that had a winning season had more fun.

One practical problem occurs in indoor soccer, however. Its growing popularity is putting pressure on the existing arenas to provide practice time for team indoor soccer practice, particularly as basketball and ice hockey often utilize the same indoor facilities. It reminded McIntosh of his college experience playing hockey, where the limited number of indoor roller hockey rinks forced the team to hold daily practice at 5:00 A.M. He recognized how impractical that would be for indoor youth soccer players and their parents, even assuming the Rec Center would be willing to open its doors that early. The other alternative would be to practice indoor soccer outdoors, weather permitting, and indoors in other enclosed facilities, such as school gymnasiums. The walls would not be there, so the team essentially would be practicing futsal, the form of indoor soccer that is normally played on indoor basketball courts. Practicing the drills that involve "off-the-wall" techniques would have to be reserved for the indoor arena practice sessions. That was the thinking behind dividing the practice techniques into two separate chapters in this book. Chapter 6, "Skills, Drills, and Games," includes the generic practice routines that can be done outside or inside; Chapter 7, "Off-the-Wall Drills," is for indoor practice in an arena equipped with walls.

However, the coauthors also recognized that the sport of soccer can be broken down into a relatively few basic skills that a properly motivated youngster can practice at home. For example, dribbling, juggling (controlling), and target shooting can be practiced outside, weather permitting, or in the garage. All that is needed is a hard surface. (Grass is not as good because the ball bounces differently on a solid surface.)

McIntosh recalled his travels in European cities, where he observed youngsters playing soccer in the streets (the original version of what Street Soccer USA now promotes in organized tournaments). He also noticed the common sight of a European youngster alone, with a soccer ball or hacky sack, practicing his juggling skills; much like an American youngster bounces a rubber ball off a wall to practice his baseball skills. Soccer is the favorite youth sport in Europe, and the children there were obviously motivated to practice their individual skills. How can an American indoor soccer coach motivate players to a regime of daily practice at home? How can that coach compete with television, video games, and other things that distract young players? In the final chapter of this book, "Winning," the coauthors deal with the subject of motivation and suggest the idea of shoulder stars, similar to the stars that some college football teams put on the helmets of players who make exceptional plays. Our experience is that young players will work hard to earn shoulder stars, so we recommend them as possible rewards for daily practice at home on the days the team does not practice. You can construct weekly home practice cards for parents to sign each day their child spends a minimum of 30 minutes practicing his or her soccer skills. Five days of home practice will earn the player a shoulder star.

The skill of "juggling" the ball with foot, head, chest, and knee can be practiced anywhere to help develop the ability to effectively control the ball.

Parents and Pressure

As mentioned above, the Little League rage problem has adversely affected the efforts of youth sports coaches. It's tough to maintain the "Keep it simple; make it fun" philosophy with "win at any cost" parents breathing down their necks. When *Managing Little League Baseball*, the first of McIntosh's three books on Little League, was published in 1985, it received a large number of reviews in the media. The chapter entitled "Parents and Pressure" received the most attention because of the growing number of reports of parental abuse of coaches, umpires, and, unfortunately, their own children, which had even escalated to acts of violence during and after games. The epitomizing example of parental rage occurred in Massachusetts several years ago, when an enraged father murdered the coach of his son's hockey team. Unfortunately the sport of youth soccer has been infected as well, with the onset of the "soccer mom" phenomenon. Some of these moms outdo their spouses in their obsession with seeing their children win. What is a young soccer player to do when two respected authority figures, his or her parent on one hand and coach on the other, are giving contrary signals? It places the kind of pressure on the child that takes the fun out of the game. Indoor soccer, with eight-foot barriers—arena walls topped by Plexiglas—has made it a little more difficult for the parents to vent their feelings directly, but that encourages some to just shout louder. In Montgomery County, Maryland, the parents and pressure problem became so acute in a particular soccer league that league officials were forced to organize a parent police force to monitor the actions of spectators and to report violators to the league. In Chapter 11 of this book, "Dealing with Parents and Pressure," we address the problem as it relates to indoor youth soccer.

In Chapter 5 we provide two snapshot views of what we believe are ideal models for indoor soccer facilities, one a private center, the Soccer Spot in Grand Rapids, Michigan, and the other a public facility in Ocean City, Maryland, operated by the Ocean City Parks and Recreation Department. The latter is not only a state-of-the-art physical plant, but also a model with respect to its philosophy of good coach, player, and parent relationships. To counter the win-at-any-cost philosophy of overaggressive parents and coaches, their approach is a play-hard-to-win philosophy, where participation trophies, rather than championship trophies, are awarded to the players who played hard to win, whether they won or not.

This book has been written with the combined efforts of an experienced and successful author of youth sports books and an experienced and successful player and father/coach of both outdoor and indoor soccer—of boys and girls. Together we represent 30 years of coaching youth sports as *volunteer coaches*. With all due respect to school coaches, we feel we can better relate to baffled parent/coaches because we have been there personally. Hopefully our joint venture will help the baffled parents whose children have persuaded them to coach. Maybe there will even be some baffled parents who will be told, as Ned McIntosh was, "We have too many kids and not enough coaches; but we can guarantee your child will play if you will agree to coach his or her team." He was told, at the Ocean City, Maryland, Recreation Complex, that the same situation he encountered in California (more kids registered than volunteer coaches to handle them) exists there as well, at the U6 (under age 6) level. (Their indoor soccer program starts at five years of age.) His research also found an indoor youth soccer program in Seattle, called Lil' Kickers, where boys and girls as young as 18 months can participate. They advertise, "We don't just teach soccer to kids, we also use soccer as a tool to teach kids about life." Those examples of very early entry of boys and girls into the indoor youth soccer phenomenon would predict that the current popularity in the sport will continue, and probably increase, in the future. That means more baffled parent/coaches.

Recognizing that many baffled parents, and others, will probably confess they don't understand the differences between outdoor and indoor soccer, we have devoted Chapter 4 to explaining the significant differences. However, with respect to the basic skills, soccer is still soccer, and many youngsters play outdoor soccer in the nice weather and indoor soccer in the cold weather. As mentioned above, Chapter 6 is devoted to the skills, drills, and games that can help develop the skills common to both outdoor and indoor soccer. Chapter 7, on the other hand, covers the drills and skills that are *unique* to indoor soccer.

The Role of the Volunteer Coach

It has been reported that 50 percent of children participating in today's youth sports live in single-parent homes, most of them with their mothers. That places volunteer male coaches in the sensitive role of being a male role model in the life of his players, in addition to all of the other positive roles he must assume: teacher, coach, and friend. A coach must guide young children physically, socially, and emotionally as they grow from childhood through adolescence.

Sometimes a coach may be cast in the role of a friend to the friendless, which means he or she has the additional responsibility of ensuring that every child feels accepted as an equal member of the team.

In Chapter 3 we give a snapshot view of two professional youth coaching organizations: the National Youth Sports Coaches' Association (NYSCA), which covers all youth sports, and the Indoor Soccer Coaches Association (ISCA), which limits itself to soccer. Both are highly professional organizations dedicated to the highest principles in volunteer coaches working with American youth, and both have training and certification programs their coaches must complete. NYSCA has a Coaches' Code of Ethics, shown in Chapter 3, which its coaches must sign.

Boys and Girls

We mentioned that indoor soccer is a popular sport for boys and girls, who play together on the same teams, particularly in the youth U12 and under leagues. A number of our pictures in this book show both boys and girls in action. Please understand that when we use either the male or female pronoun throughout the book, we are referring to both.

Thanks for Your Help

We are indebted to many people and organizations involved in indoor youth soccer for their help. They include Tom Shuster, director of Ocean City Parks and Recreation, Ocean City, Maryland, and his associates, Al "Hondo" Handy, supervisor, and Tammy Beres, administrative associate; Beverly Kennedy Hurley, office manager for coauthor Jeff Thaler; Kevin Darcy, former professional soccer player and current soccer coach and teacher at The Salisbury School; Jerry Elmer, highly regarded coach of both indoor and outdoor youth soccer; Don Shapero, president of the United States Indoor Soccer Association, who has given us a great overview of indoor youth soccer, both directly and via copies of his organization's magazine, *Goal Indoor*; Dr. Cathy Ferguson, chief marketing manager of American Youth Soccer Organization (AYSO); Brian Quinn and Ralf Wilhelms, former professional soccer players and coaches active in the Indoor Soccer Coaches Association (ISCA), who shared with us a CD-ROM and related material on coaching indoor youth soccer; Fred Engh, president of National Association of Youth Sports (NAYS), who has shared some of his organization's materials; Jeffrey Stern, president of Street Soccer USA, who provided material and pictures on that unique version of indoor soccer; Sterling Publishing Company, Inc., publisher of the English translation of *Indoor Soccer*, by Evert Teunissen, which allowed us to use material from that book; Rosen Publishing Company, which permitted us to quote from their book *The History of Soccer*; and Jan Eric Nordmo, president of Off the Wall Soccer Arena Soccer Centers, Inc.

CHAPTER 1

The World's Most Popular Youth Sport: Its Origin and History

It is doubtful that any youth sport popular today is any older in its origin than soccer. The book *The History of Soccer*, published by PowerKids Press, includes the illustration of an ancient stone carving from Rome, circa 200 B.C., showing a soccer-like ball being kicked. Soccer, as we know it today, is played throughout the world and is included as an Olympic sport for both men and women. But the recognized world championship of soccer is the World Cup.

All accounts of the history of soccer generally agree that the sport originated in England. It is well documented as being organized among English villages by the year A.D. 1000. In England, and later throughout the world, it was called football; and the first official rules of the game were drafted by students at Cambridge University in 1846. A grisly myth, not so well documented, has been handed down through the ages. It was rumored that when English sailors took pirates as prisoners during frequent Naval battles, they would chop off the pirates' heads and kick them around. For obvious reasons, that bloodcurdling myth is not widely mentioned in histories of the sport. What *is* known is that England, with its mighty fleet of sailing vessels, introduced the game of *football* to the rest of the world. When the English brought the game to the United States, however, we already had an established sport called football, so the new English sport was called associated football. The word *associated* was shortened to *assoc*, and then to *soccer*. It is not clear when the word *soccer* was adopted in the rest of the world, but the sport is still referred to in England, and other countries, as football.

Today, professional teams are organized in just about every country of the world, and every four years they compete for the ultimate award in soccer supremacy, the World Cup. Women's soccer also became very popular; the U.S. team won the women's World Cup in 1991 and 1999. When the men's World Cup tournament was held in the United States in 1994, it created a renewed interest in a sport that many Americans had considered boring due to the low-scoring games. Soccer was further recognized as an Olympic sport, and the U.S. Women's team won the first U.S. gold medal in 1996. When the U.S. men's team reached the World Cup semifinals in 2002, but lost a close game to Germany, it highlighted the U.S. interest in the sport even more. Despite the time difference, the game with Germany was carried by U.S. television, and a surprisingly large number of fans stayed up and tuned in.

In soccer, as in all sports, the youth version mirrored the growth in popularity of the professional sport. The level of interest of any subject is often measured by the number of websites devoted to it on the Internet. Using the search words *youth soccer*, we found more than 30,000 different websites! The number of national and international organizations sponsoring youth soccer is another indicator of the extent of interest. It includes the following:

United States Indoor Soccer Association (USISA)

American Youth Soccer Organization (AYSO)

United States Youth Soccer Association (USYSA)

Soccer Association for Youth (SAY)

National Alliance of Youth Sports (NAYS)

Fédération Internationale de Football Association (FIFA)

United States Soccer Federation (USSF)

Street Soccer Cup USA

The history of indoor soccer is not as easy to trace. Evert Teunissen's book *Indoor Soccer* reported the formation of the Helder Indoor Soccer Organization (HZVO) in Holland in 1963, 100 years after outdoor soccer was recognized as a sport in England. It was founded to keep players together in the winter months. There was initial opposition from some of the outdoor soccer clubs, because indoor soccer became so popular that rival players from the outdoor clubs were crossing over to play with players from other teams. The controversy was resolved when it was decided to treat indoor soccer as a different sport, not just an interim sport during the winter for outdoor soccer players. In fact, indoor soccer became recognized as a sport that could teach outdoor soccer players better individual technical skills and ball control. Much credit is given to Street Soccer, the informal game European youngsters have played for years. It is also played on a hard surface, the players can dribble, no one interferes, and the rules don't take away the fun.

Futsal, a form of indoor soccer, popular internationally, was originated in Uruguay in 1930, when a five-on-five version of soccer for youth competition was started in YMCAs. The game was played on basketball-size courts, both indoors and outdoors, but without sidewalls. Arena indoor soccer, with sidewalls, has been played professionally in the United States since the 1940s. But it was the forming of the Major Indoor Soccer League in 1978 that firmly established the indoor game as part of the U.S. sports scene. Many believe indoor soccer was created initially as a way to play the popular sport year-round, particularly in northern climates, where cold weather prevented outdoor competition during the winter months. It was considered a way to keep professional soccer players in shape physically, as well as continually sharpening their playing skills.

Because of the more restricted playing surface, indoor soccer was used initially as a convenient way to practice outdoor soccer in inclement weather, essentially for half-field practice. Scrimmage games, using fewer players, developed an interest in indoor soccer as a sport, apart from outdoor soccer, since the smaller playing surface required faster reaction time and involved more scoring. Those two features represent the elements that make indoor soccer so popular today: speed and high scoring.

The first recognized competition in futsal was sponsored in Europe by the European Soccer Union. It was like outdoor soccer in most respects but had fewer players and smaller playing areas. School gymnasiums provided a smaller space in most cases. As in outdoor soccer, the perimeter lines of the gym represented the boundaries, and there were many restarts when the ball went out of bounds. Although futsal is still played in many countries, a much more popular indoor game, arena soccer, came into its own with the formation of the United States Indoor Soccer Association. To

In Ocean City, Maryland, interest in youth soccer is great in the Tots League, for four- to six-year-olds, in the city's indoor soccer complex, organized by the Parks and Recreation Department. Note the arena walls, topped by Plexiglas, and the cushioned tile floor.

a spectator seeing it for the first time, arena soccer, with walls, appears to be a hybrid of soccer and hockey, with the ball constantly in play, as it ricochets off the arena walls. One coach calls it "pinball soccer."

In Mexico, indoor soccer is *futbol rapido*, highlighting the speed of the popular indoor game. Its popularity there, as well as in parts of Southern California and Texas, has resulted in outdoor/indoor soccer arenas, under lights. It has become a favorite evening spectator sport, as the cooler weather at night favors the arena game, even in preference to the outdoor sport. It parallels the development of professional arena football in the United States

As stated in the Introduction, the Soccer Industry Council of America conducted a survey in 2000, showing that there are more than 18 million children and adults in the United States participating in soccer, making it America's number one family sport. Of those 18 million, 76 percent are under the age of 18, and for every 10 male players there are 7 females. Since the interest in youth soccer is even stronger in other countries of the world, there can be no denying that soccer is the world's most popular youth sport.

CHAPTER 2

What Is Indoor Soccer?

In the only published book on the subject of indoor soccer, *Indoor Soccer: Tactics, Techniques, and Teamwork*, Evert Teunissen calls it "arguably the most popular sport in the world." He continues, "While other sports measure their popularity by the number of fans, indoor soccer continues to see the number of players increase." The survey of the United States Soccer Market, conducted by the Soccer Industry Council of America (see Exhibit I.1 in the Introduction) certainly confirms that soccer is America's number one family sport, and indoor youth soccer its most popular and fastest-growing segment.

In his book, Teunissen, a Dutch coach, is referring mostly to *European* indoor soccer, called futsal, which is described below. He mentions that futsal is a refinement of street soccer, the informal brand of soccer played by European youngsters but also another recognized form of indoor soccer. Both futsal and street soccer are versions of indoor soccer that are popular in the United States as well as Europe. However, the most popular form of indoor youth soccer in the United States is arena soccer. At first glance, the playing field for arena soccer looks like a hockey arena without ice, and the similarity to hockey is also obvious with respect to continuous play, ricochets off the boards, and no area designated out of bounds. The most significant difference between outdoor soccer and all versions of indoor soccer is *speed*. The smaller playing surface alone dictates faster play, and the addition of dasher walls in arena soccer adds a new dimension to the game. The indoor game is fast-paced, with more frequent scoring. There is no opportunity for leisurely advancing the ball up the field as in outdoor soccer, since one good kick toward the opposite goal can change the mode immediately from defense to offense, because of the shorter playing area. And there is no opportunity for quick rest periods during resets, as is common in outdoor soccer, where out-of-bounds balls are chased, substitutions are allowed, and resets are started. Instead of going out of bounds, the ball, in indoor soccer, ricochets against the wall and returns to the playing surface. Play continues without interruption.

Teunissen points out that technique, performance, and speed are the essential ingredients of indoor soccer. Dribbling, passing, and ball control are the main technical elements. The instep and head shots are less common when trying to score goals. "This is why in indoor soccer practice, for both individuals and the group, players must work on situations oriented toward the goal," he adds. "Dribbling, feinting, accurate ball passing, increasing speed, cutting, and turning require much practice and regularity until the player's skills become automatic," he adds. With regard to passing, the second important technique in indoor soccer, Teunissen points out, "Passing the ball to a teammate is a specific action requiring execution speed, ball speed, and accuracy so that the ball reaches the teammates' feet at the right moment and in the same direction he is turning. Players need to be able to do this with the inside or outside of the foot." Controlling is the final of the three important techniques required of an indoor soccer player. Teunissen notes, "Controlling a ball that reaches the player at a fast speed requires the player to reduce the speed of the ball (but not stop it) and take it in one movement to an open space to continue the game. The player should be able to do this with both feet and with both the inside and outside of the foot."

All four versions of indoor soccer (described below) are similar, in comparison to outdoor soccer, in that the playing field is smaller and the number of players on a team fewer. It is interesting to note there is also some indoor soccer played *outdoors*, principally in Southern California, Texas, and Mexico. Even where the weather would permit playing soccer outdoors, some leagues, intrigued by the unique features of arena indoor soccer, have constructed outdoor arenas with walls, and typically schedule their games under lights in the evening when the temperatures are cooler. In Mexico, the outdoor version of indoor soccer is called *futbol rapido*, which highlights the speed of the game. Street Soccer Cup tournaments, for four-on-four teams, are frequently held in portable arenas that are set up and taken down, outdoors as well as indoors.

"We are like a traveling circus," says Jeffrey Stern, president of Street Soccer Cup USA, in describing the wide variety of venues in which Street Soccer tournaments are held. Street Soccer's slogan is "Score More, Four on Four," highlighting the high-scoring feature of indoor soccer. The following outline provides a description of the four forms of indoor soccer currently popular in the United States.

Arena Indoor Soccer

The most popular of the four forms of indoor soccer is arena soccer. Spectators, viewing arena indoor soccer for the first time sometimes call it pinball soccer, because of the way the ball is deliberately played off the walls. It is also frequently called hockey without the ice.

In the United States there are now more than 500 privately owned indoor facilities where arena-style indoor soccer is played, and each facility houses at least two indoor soccer arenas; some have as many as six. That means more than 1,000 arenas, just in the private sector. Some are converted indoor tennis structures, and many are able to convert the playing areas for various indoor sports in addition to soccer, such as basketball, tennis, roller hockey, handball, etc.

In addition to the commercial facilities, there are innumerable other public facilities for indoor soccer, including YMCAs, schools, and city recreation complexes. Chapter 5 profiles one of those facilities as a model, the Ocean City, Maryland, Municipal Recreation Complex, with two indoor soccer arenas, the newest a state-of-the-art field of play. And within a 20-mile radius of that building there is a YMCA with two arenas and a privately owned facility in Salisbury, Maryland, also with two arenas. Although these indoor complexes sponsor leagues of all ages and genders, the primary emphasis is on indoor youth soccer, for players from 5 to 18 years old. For the relatively small geographic area on the Eastern Shore of Maryland to offer six indoor soccer arenas is another indication of the growing popularity of this youth sport. In Seattle, the Lil' Kickers program enrolls children as young as 18 months. When they reach U12 level, they will be seasoned veterans of indoor youth soccer.

The United States Indoor Soccer Association has taken the leadership in promoting arena soccer, from the youth level to the professional level. It

With the dasher boards in the background and a solid surface instead of grass, indoor arena soccer is a faster, higher-scoring game.

Photo courtesy of Street Soccer Cup USA.

publishes the only magazine devoted to indoor soccer, *Goal Indoor*. It also publishes two versions of the Official Rules of Indoor Soccer, one the professional set of rules, and the other the Youth and Amateur book. Chapter 10 provides a review of the most significant of the rules in the Youth and Amateur book.

Indoor soccer, of course, is like outdoor soccer in many respects. The basic skills of dribbling, passing, and receiving, controlling the ball, heading, and goaltending are the same. But as Teunissen points out, the level of competence in those skills is higher in indoor soccer, because the playing area is smaller, reaction time quicker, and the opportunities to score greater. Indoor soccer is a much faster-paced game because of the smaller playing field, fewer players on a team, continuous play, and substituting on the run, as is done in hockey. The dasher boards create different strategy skills in indoor soccer, as the players learn to use them as additional players, on both offense and defense. A more complete analysis of the differences between outdoor and indoor soccer is presented in Chapter 4.

Street Soccer

When coauthor Ned McIntosh traveled in Europe, he was intrigued by the informal games of soccer he saw youngsters playing in the streets of nearly every city. "In America," he noted, "if you throw a ball to a kid, he will catch it in his hands; in Europe, whether it is a hacky sack, a rubber ball, or

Action in a Street Soccer Cup USA tournament is fast, with only a goalie and three players on each team. "Score More with Four on Four" is the slogan. Photo courtesy of Street Soccer Cup USA.

a soccer ball, he will catch it with his foot and begin dribbling." So it is no surprise that organized street soccer had its origin in Europe. Last year, more than 300,000 players from 42 countries hit the streets and competed in street soccer tournaments sponsored by Street Soccer Cup USA.

Leave it to American ingenuity to develop a program to market street soccer road shows in seven metropolitan cities across the United States for annual Street Soccer Cup USA tournaments. Teams consist of one goalie and three field players, with one substitute recommended because of the fast pace of the game. Walled courts 66 feet by 46 feet are transported by truck to provide eight to ten courts for a tournament.

Skill contests in soccer, as well as non-soccer games, such as water wars, are also staged as side events at Street Soccer Cup tournaments. Street Soccer Cup USA youth age-groups are U8, U10, U12, U14, U16, and U18. There are also adult participation categories, including men's, women's, and co-ed. For more information about Street Soccer Cup tournaments, log onto the website at www.streetsoccercup.com.

Futsal

The origin of youth futsal can be traced back to Uruguay in 1930, when a five-on-five version of indoor soccer was devised for youth competition in YMCAs. Futsal is the international term for the game, a combination of the Spanish word for "soccer," *FUTbol*, and the French word for "indoor," *SALon*. Futsal quickly gained popularity throughout South America, particularly in Brazil. The skill developed in this game is visible in the world-famous style the Brazilians display, both outdoors and indoors. Brazilian superstars like Pele, Zico, Socrates, and Bebeto developed their skill playing futsal. Brazil has consistently produced the dominant team in professional competition, and the game is now sponsored by the Fédération Internationale de Football Association (FIFA) all over the world, including Europe; North, Central, and South America; Africa; and Asia.

The U.S. Futsal Federation was incorporated in 1981, and has grown to an organization of 40,000 members, most of whom are under 19 years of age. The game is frequently referred to as five on five, and is usually played on basketball-size courts without the use of dasher board walls. In this respect it is like outdoor soccer, with out-of-bounds lines stopping play. U.S. Futsal has conducted a national championship each year since 1985. Its youth level was strengthened when the Boys and Girls Clubs of America adopted the sport, which is now played at about 1,100 of that organization's venues throughout the United States. The American Youth Soccer Organization (AYSO) also signed an agreement in 1995 to promote futsal, under the auspices of U.S. Futsal. USSF is also working to affiliate with the YMCA, NCAA, National High School Association of America, and the National Junior College Association; estimates indicate that there are approximately 112,000 players participating in this sport in the United States.

Futsal, in contrast to the other two forms of indoor soccer, uses a special low-bounce ball, necessitating players to use their skills, rather than the ball's bounce, to propel it. Street Soccer and Indoor Arena soccer use the same size ball as outdoor soccer, as dictated by age-group.

For more information about futsal in the United States, log onto the website of the United States Futsal Federation, www.futsal.com

SocCourt (Wall Soccer)

The newest development of a youth sport, using a soccer ball, is called SocCourt, or wall soccer. The slogan on its logo, "Soccer Meets Racquetball," gives you a pretty clear idea as to what it is, a one-on-one skills game

In a SocCourt drill, two players team up facing a wall and use racquetball scoring to determine who is better at controlling the ball.

that is a cross between the two sports of soccer and racquetball, with some similarities to handball, as there are no racquets. It's played on a racquetball-size court, but instead of using rackets to return the ball, you use your body (excluding the hands). The other major difference is you have up to two bounces to return the ball (floor and/or body bounces).

Arena indoor soccer coaches have adopted the one-on-one feature of SocCourt as a competitive drill. Players pair off along the walls of the arena and compete. This allows them to sharpen their reaction time to wall bounces, and their kicking accuracy within a confined space. The drill can become more fun when the coach sets up a SocCourt tournament among his players, with the winning player getting a token prize, such as a headband in the team colors.

To further promote the sport, the American Wall Soccer Association (AWSA) has been organized to promote and develop Wall Soccer into a worldwide sport. It is dedicated to the development of kids' programs and competition. The first annual Wall Soccer Nationals was held in San Diego in March 2000. It was an open tournament, and first place went to Shawn Beyer, a professional indoor soccer star with the San Diego Sockers, but third place was snagged by a high school player, Kevin Noonan. Shawn Beyer was quoted as saying, "I kicked a ball against the garage door at my house since I was five years old. It helped me to develop many skills that I've needed on the field." It is interesting that he mentions his fascination with practicing soccer alone, something European young-sters still do. Few American kids practice alone, perhaps because there are so many other things competing for their attention.

Tony Klarich, the organizer of the sport of SocCourt, is a good profes-sional soccer player and professional water skier. He has organized more than 200 water sports tournaments, and he envisions the first Wall Soccer Tournament paving the way for similar promotional success for this unique sport. During the development stage of the sport, new members can join free of charge. They will receive a newsletter, a league development guide, and discounts on AWSA merchandise, by logging onto the website at www.SocCourt.com.

Indoor Youth Soccer Organizations

There are a surprisingly large number of organizations involved in promoting indoor youth soccer. Some are youth sports organizations that promote indoor soccer exclusively; some promote both indoor and outdoor soccer; some are involved in a variety of youth sports; some are soccer officials' organizations; and some promote the development of arenas for indoor soccer, as well as other indoor sports.

The increase of indoor sports facilities has mirrored the growth of indoor soccer, mushrooming from less than 100 indoor sports buildings five years ago to more than 500 in 2002, each facility housing at least two arenas.

Indoor Soccer Organizations

The leading organization sponsoring indoor soccer exclusively is the United States Indoor Soccer Association (USISA), which publishes the only magazine entirely devoted to indoor soccer, *Goal Indoor*. USISA's purpose is to promote indoor soccer, from the professional level to the youth level, and it currently claims 1.8 million members. It is also active in the development of facilities throughout the country for the housing of indoor soccer arenas. Its unique, eye-catching logo was created by founder and president Don Shapero. The colorful red, white, and blue design reflects the widespread appeal of indoor soccer throughout the United States. The three stars, which run diagonally across the image of the shield, represent the youth, amateur, and professional levels of play. The four horizontal red lines symbolize the four regions of the country where indoor soccer is played.

The USISA sponsors leagues and tournaments at all levels. It publishes "The Official Rules of Indoor Soccer," in two editions: Professional, and Youth and Amateur. With USISA's permission, we have reprinted the key rules for youth soccer in Chapter 10. For more information about USISA, you may write Don Shapero, President, USISA, P.O.

Box 6569, Arlington, VA 22206-0569; call (703) 820-2810; or log onto the website at www.usindoor.com.

The U.S. Futsal Federation was incorporated in 1983 and has conducted a National Championship annually since 1985. It gave indoor youth soccer a big boost when it affiliated with two national organizations, the Boys and Girls Clubs of America and the U.S. Youth Soccer Association in 1995. For more information about the U.S. Futsal Federation, log onto the website at www.futsal.org.

The American Youth Soccer Organization (AYSO) is the largest youth soccer association in the country, with nearly 630,000 boys and girls 4 to 18 years old and 250,000 volunteer coaches, referees, and administrators in 46 states. Although they do not break down their statistics with respect to players who play outdoor soccer, indoor soccer, or both, they concur that the popularity of indoor soccer is growing. The organization's home base is in California. For more information you may write to American Youth Soccer Organization, 12501 A. Isis Ave., Hawthorne, CA 90250; phone (800) 872-2976; or visit the website at www.soccer.org.

The oldest and most distinguished international soccer organization is Fédération Internationale de Football Association (FIFA). It was founded in 1904 and is the sponsor of the World Cup for professional soccer. The United States joined the organization in 1913. The first World Cup was held in 1930. By the year 2000, the organization had grown to 204 countries, making it one of the biggest and most popular sports federations in the world. FIFA dedicated the 2002 World cup to children under the banner of "Say Yes for Children." You may contact FIFA by logging onto the website at www.fifa.com.

Additional organizations involved directly or indirectly with indoor youth soccer include the following:

- National Alliance for Youth Sports (NAYS): This is the premier youth sports organization in the country, not just for youth soccer, but for all youth sports. Better than any other, it addresses the growing concern for making participation in youth sports a positive experience and condemns the winning-is-everything mentality. Its founder and president, Fred Engh, wrote a landmark book, *Why Johnny Hates Sports*, which exposed the negative methods and attitudes of some coaches and parents that were taking away the fun of participating. The organization's positive program for coaches includes training and certification. (A copy of sample questions in the certification exam is shown in Chapter 5.) The implementation of its constructive program is embodied in two codes of ethics they ask coaches and parents to sign. The codes commit participants to the same philosophy this book embraces with respect to indoor youth soccer, i.e., "Keep it simple; make it fun." NAYS sponsors the National Youth Sports Coaches Association, which is described later in this chapter. The "Coaches' Code of Ethics" is shown in that section. NAYS also sponsors the Parents Association for Youth Sports (PAYS). For more information about National Alliance of Youth Sports, log onto the website at www.nays.org.

- Parents Association for Youth Sports (PAYS): This is a unique association in that it is the only one for parents involved in out-of-school youth sports. Their program educates and motivates youth league parents to make their children's sports experience safe and meaningful. PAYS encourages good sportsmanship, positive reinforcement, and proper perspective. Its goal is to stop negative parent behavior before it happens. Parents who are interested in becoming PAYS members must attend a 30-minute clinic, conducted by representatives of their local NAYS chapter. They view a training video, participate in discussion with other parents, and sign the "Parent's Code of Ethics" (shown in Chapter 11). All parents are given positive-slogan buttons to wear at games to remind themselves and other parents to demonstrate good sportsmanship. To learn more about PAYS, call 800-688-KIDS, or visit the NAYS website at www.nays.org to find out how to establish a PAYS program for your league or community.

- United States Youth Soccer Association (USYSA): Approximately 3 million players between the ages of 5 and 19 are registered within this network of 55 state associations. Programs are administered with the help of more than 300,000 coaches and 500,000 volunteers. They sponsor national championships at all youth levels. The organization's headquarters are in Richardson, Texas. To learn more, visit www.usysa.org.

- Soccer Association for Youth, USA: This association is strongest in the northern states, where indoor soccer is very popular, and the outdoor season relatively short because of weather. It claims more than 100,000 kids between the ages of 4 and 18 enrolled across the country. The states with the largest number of members are Ohio, Wisconsin, Indiana, Pennsylvania, and New York. For more information, visit www.saysoccer.org.

- United States Soccer Federation (USSF): This is the governing body of soccer in all its forms within the United States, which has helped chart the course for the sport in the United States for 88 years. It is affiliated with FIFA and served as the host federation for World Cup USA in 1994. For more information, visit www.us-soccer.com.

- Street Soccer Cup USA: This is an international organization that sponsors four-on-four tournaments in major U.S. cities (seven cities in 2000.) Teams consist of three players and a goalie (plus one substitute), and competition is set up for all age levels starting with U8. Consequently, teams can be formed from existing teams of either indoor or outdoor leagues, although indoor teams will have an advantage, as the competition is staged in indoor-like courts. Games are played on specially manu-

Indoor soccer is popular as a co-ed youth sport, particularly in the U12 age range. This girl is participating in one of the tournaments sponsored by Street Soccer Cup USA. Photo courtesy of Street Soccer Cup USA.

factured walled courts 66 feet by 46 feet with solid surface. In the year 2000, more than 300,000 players from 42 countries around the world competed.

Street Soccer Cup USA is responsible for promoting the tournaments and handles all arrangements, including erecting the arenas for play. For more information, contact info@streetsoccercup.com.

• SocCourt (Wall Soccer): SocCourt is the newest form of indoor soccer, and the most important one in terms of the refinement of individual soccer skills, as it offers one-on-one competition. For all the young soccer players who practice their soccer skills alone by kicking a ball against a garage door, this is the sport for them. It is a combination of soccer and handball in a small court about the size of a handball court. The hands are not allowed, but any other part of the body is, as the players compete by bouncing the ball against a wall, with the other player handling the ricochet. Unlike handball, two bounces are allowed on the body (for example, head and foot). It suggests a good indoor soccer drill. Those interested in more information about this fledgling sport should send an E-mail to info@SocCourt.com.

Indoor Soccer Arena Companies

The following two private sector organizations, the Federation of Sports Arenas and Let's Play Sports, Inc., have a collateral relationship to youth indoor soccer.

The Federation of Sports Arenas (FSA) is a national soccer association, comprised of individual arenas competing against each other in men's and women's open divisions, and boys' and girls' divisions ranging from U12 to U18. All tournaments and league play eventually lead to playoffs and a national champion for each age group. For more information go to the website at www.arenaleague.com.

Let's Play Sports, Inc., is a low-cost source of indoor sports facilities. The facilities are designed and built specifically for the players. It provides dependable, responsive management to operate the facilities with cost-effective services to enhance the enjoyment of the people living in the communities served. Let's Play Sports, Inc., currently owns and operates 15 sports facilities in eight states and has additional facilities in various stages of development and/or acquisition. In many locales, Let's Play Sports acts as a parks department or recreation center. The focus is strongly on indoor soccer, and the organization has created a comprehensive indoor soccer rulebook, which can be downloaded from www.letsplaysoccer.com.

Indoor Soccer Coaches Organizations

There are two distinguished national coaches organizations involved in assuring a positive approach to the officiating of youth indoor soccer. The National Youth Sports Coaches Association (NYSCA) has 2,500 chapters in 50 states and on U.S. military bases internationally. It is affiliated with the National Alliance of Youth Sports (NAYS). Its main goal is to sensitize coaches and parents to assume their responsibilities toward making the participation in youth sports a positive experience for children. Through their sponsored National Youth Sports Coaches Association (NYSCA) they provide training, support, and continuing education to adults who volunteer to coach out-of-school youth sports teams. Around 1.3 million individuals have become NYSCA-certified coaches since the program began in 1981. Coaches must sign a Coaches' Code of Ethics (see Exhibit 3.1). The organization's main goal is to provide coaches with the knowledge necessary to coach the youth of our country, be it soccer, Little League baseball, or any other youth sport. NYSCA offers a satisfying training program with easy-to-reach goals, and a final exam to show what has been learned. Coauthor Jeff Thaler is a member and certified coach.

It was not a coincidence that one of NAYS' affiliates, the Ocean City, Maryland, Recreation Complex, was chosen as the venue for this book, nor that Jeff Thaler, one of its certified coaches, was chosen as coauthor. The organization's coaching philosophy is consistent with the theme of this book, with respect to coaching children: "Keep it simple; make it fun." One of the benefits of membership is a subscription to the organization's *Youth Sports Journal*, which provides helpful coaching tips. More information is available at www.NAYS.org.

Another well-known coaches organization is the Indoor Soccer Coaches Association (ISCA). ISCA was formed to promote, educate, provide service, and generate interest in the game of indoor soccer. The objective is to provide potential coaches a better knowledge of the game, a greater appreciation of the techniques and tactics, and an enhanced appreciation of the physical and psychological demands of indoor soccer. It is dedicated to the development of the youth soccer player. ISCA has a national coaching licensing program that presents coaches with the theoretical, technical, and practical aspects of coaching. When a coach completes all three components at the indoor youth soccer level, he or she becomes formally licensed. Brian Quinn and Ralf Wilhelms, prominent members of ISCA, have produced a CD-ROM on coaching indoor youth soccer; it

Coaches' Code of Ethics

I hereby pledge to live up to my certification as an NYSCA coach by following the NYSCA Coaches' Code of Ethics.

- I will place the emotional and physical well-being of my players ahead of a personal desire to win.

- I will treat each player as an individual, remembering the large range of emotional and physical development for the same age-group.

- I will do my best to provide a safe playing situation for my players.

- I will promise to review and practice the basic first aid principles needed to treat injuries of my players.

- I will do my best to organize practices that are fun and challenging for my players.

- I will lead by example in demonstrating fair play and sportsmanship to all my players.

- I will provide a sports environment for my team that is free of drugs, tobacco, and alcohol, and I will refrain from their use at all youth sports events.

- I will be knowledgeable in the rules of each sport that I coach, and I will teach these rules to my players.

- I will use those coaching techniques appropriate for each of the skills that I teach.

- I will remember that I am a youth sports coach, and that the game is for children and not adults.

_____

Coach Signature   Date

EXHIBIT 3.1   NYSCA Coaches' Code of Ethics

comes with booklets with diagrams and a copy of the coaches test. Both men are eminently qualified professionals. Quinn is an eight-time all-star midfielder, and Wilhelms is a two-time national indoor champion. For more information about ISCA, its licensing program, and/or its training aids, log onto the website at www.isca.net.

CHAPTER 4

Differences Between Indoor and Outdoor Soccer

In terms of size, there are three obvious differences between indoor and outdoor soccer, that is, the size of the playing surface, the size of the goals, and the size of the teams (number of players). The official size of an outdoor soccer field is a rectangle, 110 yards by 65 yards, somewhat larger than a football field. The much smaller surface of an indoor soccer arena is a standard 60 yards by 25 yards, with corners rounded in the arc of a circle with a 28-foot radius and sidewalls 8 feet high. The preferred outdoor surface is grass. Indoor arena surfaces vary from artificial grass to the much-preferred cushioned tile, where players use indoor soccer rubber-soled shoes or sneakers. Indoor soccer has become so popular that athletic stores now carry soccer cleats for outdoor play and indoor soccer shoes for indoor play.

The size of the goals varies significantly. A full-size outdoor goal is 8 yards wide by 8 feet high; an indoor goal is 4 yards wide—half the width of the outdoor goal—and 6½ feet high. The smaller goal in indoor soccer sends an obvious message to indoor soccer players: they must be more skilled and more accurate in their shooting skills than they would need to be in outdoor soccer. Everyone plays offense in indoor soccer. When the team gains control of the ball, players who play strictly defense in the outdoor sport must practice and perfect their ability to shoot on goal in indoor soccer. Shooting with both right and left feet is also required, since the fast pace of the game will not allow specialists from the right or left side of the playing area.

The size of the teams varies from 11 on an outdoor soccer team to from 5 to 7 players on an indoor team. An indoor team of 7 would, in addition to the goalie, include two forwards, one midfielder, one sweeper, and two defenders. Indoor soccer has one player called the sweeper. This player is usually one of the stronger players. The sweeper plays both offense and defense—he or she is the playmaker on offense and is usually used for defensively marking (face checking) a key player on the other team on defense.

This typical U12 indoor soccer team, playing in the Ocean City Rec League, consists of six players, plus a goalie.

In his book *Coaching Youth Soccer* (outdoor version), author Bobby Clark acknowledges the disadvantages in trying to coach 11 players in outdoor soccer. He says, "Fewer kids get to touch the ball—some kids in an 11-on-11 game *never* will." He goes on to recommend, even in outdoor soccer training of younger players, that a modified half-field be used, with seven players on a team, the same as the approximate standard field size and number of players for indoor soccer. Because the play is concentrated in a much smaller area, it is inconceivable that an indoor soccer player would never touch the ball.

To a spectator watching his or her first indoor soccer game after having seen outdoor youth games, speed of play is probably the most noticeable difference between the two. There are often interminable delays in the outdoor game, as the ball, which goes out of bounds frequently, must to be recovered and reset for a throw-in. In an indoor soccer game, the play is virtually uninterrupted, as the ball bounces off the side walls and back walls, instead of going out of bounds. Every player on an indoor team touches the ball frequently. There is no such thing as being on the field of play and not being involved.

Indoor soccer players usually get enough playing time to satisfy the player, or the player's parents, because the tiring pace of the game requires frequent substitutions. These substitutions are made on the run, or after goals, as in hockey, to allow the game to continue uninterrupted. In addi-

The player with the ball appears trapped between two opponents but can pivot and bank the ball against the wall to a teammate and thereby maintain control of the ball for his team.

tion, throw-ins don't exist in indoor soccer. If the ball goes above the wall and makes contact with the net, the result is a free kick. The location of the kick depends on if the ball went off the net by the goal, on the sides, or by the ceiling.

The same size ball, either number 4 or number 5, is used in both outdoor and indoor soccer. The only exception is in indoor futsal, where a soft-bounce number 4 ball is used. This minimizes the number of out-of-bounds balls, which as in outdoor soccer, stops the game.

Differences in Equipment

With the exception of shoes, the equipment for indoor soccer is essentially the same as that for outdoor soccer. Shoes with cleats are only for outdoor soccer, while good traction flat-soled shoes are preferred for indoor soccer. Indoor soccer playing areas can vary considerably—from slippery to rough. Players must adapt by controlling their bodies and using the right kind of shoes. Most injuries occur because of shoes that have inadequate soles, lack ankle support, are the wrong size, or lack cushioning. Parents are advised to buy their children shoes that are comfortable and well suited to indoor soccer. Most sports arenas do not accept shoes with black soles, because the carbon in the rubber can mark the floor. White rubber soles seem to be the most popular, and they do not mark the floor. Natural rubber soles do not wear out as fast, but they are rougher on the feet. Synthetic soles are strong and look good, but they are very sensitive to the surface temperature and dangerous if the floor is moist. Surface patterns of the soles vary a great deal. This is mostly a matter of personal preference. Professional indoor soccer players prefer suede shoes, because they are rough, which makes it easier to control the ball. Following are suggested guidelines for buying indoor soccer shoes that are comfortable and safe:

- The sole, either rubber or synthetic, must adapt well to the floor.
- The shoe must provide good heel support to protect the ankles and at the same time allow for mobility in the game.
- The back edges cannot be too rounded; they must protect the ankles and avoid pressure.
- The shoes must have enough foot room, allowing for perspiration and preferably be without nylon to avoid blisters.
- They must have a good tongue to avoid the pressure.
- The shoes cannot be too thin or the shoes won't provide enough ankle support.
- They should be the proper size, not too wide (to avoid blisters), but long enough to allow room for the feet to swell when they heat up.
- They must have well-tied laces. If they are not properly tied, shoe laces can be a problem when kicking the ball.
- There must be enough room for the toes.

A player should always wear shin guards. Although these may not be very comfortable at first and may not be considered "cool," they will protect against the inevitable accidental kicks in the shins or ankles.

Since play is indoors, lightweight clothes are suggested. Loose-fitting shorts will allow for complete freedom of leg movement.

Differences in Strategy

Generally, strategies are similar in both outdoor and indoor, except for the use of the wall in indoor soccer, which creates different angled shots and crosses. On the other hand, the larger field and no ceiling allow outdoor players the opportunity to kick the ball a long distance to clear an area. As mentioned earlier, the smaller field, smaller goal, dasher walls, and fewer players combine to create a greater sense of urgency on the part of the players. They must react more quickly to changes in the dynamics of the game. That means the indoor soccer player has to sharpen his or her short-passing skills and play toward the open space more than an outdoor soccer player does.

Indoor soccer is more interesting for the spectators. They are closer to the action in the smaller area of a soccer arena, and they tend to get much more involved in the game.

In an interview in a recent issue of *Goal Indoor*, Rasool Faily, owner of Hat Trick Indoor Soccer in Oklahoma City, had this to say: "You have a totally different perspective of the game when you play indoors. You're always surrounded by something going on; you're always involved. Obviously, you touch the ball a lot more, whereas kids playing outdoors go long stretches without touching the ball. In indoor soccer everyone's involved. Because space is very limited, whatever position you're in, you have less time to execute. You're used to being under pressure. So you don't have time to get lazy; you need to make decisions straight away."

Rasool also pointed out the weather advantage of playing in a controlled environment. "There is no wind, no rain, no sun, no snow. Any parent who has patrolled the sidelines of the outdoor game will appreciate that difference. And that is important, not just from the point of view of physical comfort. If you play [indoors] on a perfect field in perfect conditions, you have an environment that enables you to play a technically sound game. You have the controlled weather to work on short-passing ability, controlling the ball, first-touch opportunities." He could have added that no indoor games are ever called off or postponed because of the weather.

"Let's face it," he continued, "you can play a decent game outdoors, even if you have a lousy touch. But in the indoor game you have a perfect and involving environment that is less forgiving of such mistakes. For me, that makes the indoor game a more demanding sport than outdoor soccer."

In the same issue of *Goal Indoor*, Arnold Zirkes, marketing director of The Soccer Spot in Grand Rapids and Holland, Michigan, weighs in with this observation:

"Indoor soccer is a 'fun' game—it's human pinball. In the outdoor game kids wait to get in; they sit on the bench waiting for a dead ball, waiting for another kid to tire. But how quickly do you tire in the outdoor game, 11 versus 11, when you don't have to run all that much? The indoor game is faster, has more substitutions, more playing time, more touches on the ball. Indoor soccer is technically a different game, a valid game. If we just remember that for kids it can be fun, we're serving our audience." He went on to quote a study indicating the average age of a kid quitting outdoor soccer had dropped from 13 to 12; the primary reason the study gave that it wasn't fun anymore.

Jerry Elmer is a well-known youth soccer coach on the Eastern Shore of Maryland. He coaches both sports, which makes him eminently qualified to compare them. Also a coach of youth basketball, he makes an interesting analogy between that sport and indoor soccer. "When I coach an indoor game, I look at it as a basketball game with your feet. I try to match my fastest player against my opponent's best player. If he can stay focused and be successful we should win the game. The hardest thing to teach my players is to play a total man-to-man game. There is no difference between an offensive and defensive player; every player is both. As in a basketball game, when we have possession of the ball, they are all offensive players. Of course, when our opponents have possession of the ball they are all defensive players, and each has a certain man to cover. For the team to be successful, every player on our team must contain the player he is assigned to on the other team. Since you can substitute on the fly, I can make adjustments during the game if I feel the matchups aren't working. The players, however, must stay alert and recognize their assignments can change when the other team makes substitutions. This can confuse younger players, but as the season progresses this is something they learn. Outdoor, on the other hand, is a zone style of play. To the uninformed spectator or the inexperienced player, the games may seem the same. But to the knowledgeable coach, player, or spectator, the games are completely different."

Kevin Darcy, former professional soccer player in the United Soccer League, has played and coached both outdoor and indoor soccer, and conducts many clinics for indoor youth soccer. One of his most popular clinics is during Christmas week at the Ocean City Recreation Complex. It is described in the next chapter. Commenting on the advantages of indoor soccer, over outdoor, he says, "Arena soccer is higher scoring, quicker, and faster, which relates more to the American sports fan. The benefits of indoor soccer are: more touches on the ball, and if played properly, the development of quick combinations and patterns of play. Since arena soccer is played with fewer numbers, it forces involvement and can promote creativity and technical skill. One drawback is that players with deficiencies tend to get exposed easier, since all players are involved and one can get isolated in a one-on-one situation."

Darcy goes on to say, "Depending on the personnel of your team, you may benefit from playing fast and direct, or you may benefit from slowing the tempo of a match and possessing the ball. The key is to vary your attack so you are not predictable to your opponent. A team that attempts to play long straight through balls is easily defended by a well-organized defense. Consider playing a few wide balls to stretch the defense, and then play through, or over the top, to a speedy forward. Many modern-day teams tend to defend with numbers [players immediately getting behind the ball when losing possession] and upon winning the ball play quick and direct counter-attacks into deep targets [forwards], or speedy wingers."

"The key," Darcy concludes, "is identifying a style of play that suits your personnel, and varying your attack to keep your opposing team off balance. I for one love fast players, especially in defense and up-front, but I think the key is to have players who understand their roles and playmakers who understand the importance of tempo. Although as a player, I enjoy arena indoor soccer, futsal is another great alternative for a winter indoor sport. It is played within the lines of a basketball court and uses a low-bounce ball for control." Darcy is director of the ProSoccer Academy, and soccer coach of Salisbury School, both in Salisbury, Maryland.

The other significant difference between outdoor and indoor soccer is the scoring. Most observers agree the primary reason the sport of soccer was so slow catching on in the United States is because it was boring. It took a real soccer aficionado to appreciate the nuances of soccer, after sitting for two hours watching a game that ended with a 1–0 score. Indoor soccer is never boring. It's fun, which may be the reason it is growing so popular among kids and parents. Our job as coaches is to make sure it continues to be fun.

CHAPTER 5

Model Indoor Youth Soccer Facilities

One measure of the popularity and growth of indoor youth soccer has been the burgeoning number of public and private facilities that have sprung around the country. Kevin Milliken, president of the Federation of Sports Arenas, reported that in 1995 there were fewer than 100 facilities in the United States; by 2002 there were 501 privately owned and operated indoor soccer facilities, with the number increasing at a rate of 10 percent each year. The private arenas range in size from converted former indoor tennis courts, to huge multipurpose complexes, like RexFlex in Elizabeth, New Jersey. In addition to housing four indoor soccer arenas, it also has two roller hockey rinks, two NBA regulation professional basketball courts, also used for volleyball, the largest skate park in the New York–New Jersey metropolitan area, and a state-of-the art fitness center.

The imposing entrance to The Soccer Spot in Grand Rapids, Michigan

The average-size private facility houses a minimum of two 180-foot-by-80-foot indoor soccer arenas, and has an average of 3,500 members using the facilities weekly, over 50 percent of whom are indoor youth soccer players under the age of 18. A model of the private facilities devoted primarily to indoor soccer is The Soccer Spot in Grand Rapids, Michigan. Built three years ago, it houses three arenas. It is owned and operated by Josh Sheldon, who also owns a sister facility in Holland, Michigan, which was built eight years ago and houses two arenas.

According to Sheldon, 500 indoor youth soccer teams play in The Soccer Spot; which means the facility involves more than 7,000 youngsters. He conducts three indoor league schedules in the fall/winter; but he has a total of eight sessions, over the course of the year, including instructional classes.

Along with the growth of privately owned facilities there has been an equally notable rise of community public facilities for indoor youth soccer. They also vary widely in size and types—from school, YMCA, and Boys and Girls Club gymnasiums to community recreation complexes that rival the private facilities. Some purists claim that true indoor soccer must have dasher boards; they claim that all other formats, such as school gymnasiums, are not *indoor soccer*, but *soccer played indoors*. They would dismiss futsal, for example, as being indoor soccer. It is doubtful that a parent, when asked to coach his or her child's team, would understand the subtle difference between indoor soccer and soccer played indoors, nor would he or she really care. Naturally the techniques would differ, as players in arenas with dasher boards use them the way they would use an additional player, by ricocheting the ball. Many public facilities use portable dasher boards, but futsal, which preceded arena indoor soccer, will always be a unique type of indoor soccer popular with its devotees. To give recognition to all types of indoor soccer, we provide two chapters to cover drills and strategies. Chapter 6 includes those that are generic to all forms of youth soccer: outdoor, indoor arena soccer, and indoor soccer without dasher boards. Chapter 7 concentrates on the drills and strategies for arena indoor soccer with dasher boards.

A model public community facility is the Ocean City, Maryland, complex, managed by the Ocean City Parks and Recreation Department. It houses two full-size indoor soccer arenas in a 50,000-square-foot building. The newest wing was built solely for indoor arena soccer; it's a state-of-the-art facility with a new cushioned safety floor (Sport Court suspended tile), Plexiglas dasher walls and ample bleachers and viewing space for spectators. The entrance to the Ocean City Recreation Complex is shown in the photograph on page 29.

The indoor youth soccer program at Ocean City Rec started in the late 1980s and has grown to service more than 600 children. The institution practices the philosophy of "everyone plays" to ensure fair participation for players of every talent level. Individual skill development is encouraged and playing hard to win is stressed over winning. Their program's goals are:

- To help players develop skills and knowledge of the game of soccer.
- To teach good sportsmanship and healthy attitude toward competition; i.e., to discourage the win-at-any-cost attitude.
- To provide an enjoyable experience for youth and teens.

This is the entrance to the newest wing of the 50,000-square-foot Ocean City Recreation Complex, which houses two indoor soccer arenas.

- To assist in the development of self-reliance and emotional stability.
- To increase social growth: learning to get along with others and cooperate as a team.
- To help players set and attain individual goals.
- To encourage lifetime involvement in sports and physical activity.

The indoor program starts about mid-November, with the first of three training meetings for coaches. The first is a get-together so the Recreation Department can see how many volunteer coaches they have for each age group, and to assess their ability and experience. Equally important to skill training is the program's coaching philosophy. It is affiliated with the national youth sports organization, the National Alliance for Youth Sports (NAYS), renowned for its high standards of sportsmanship and coaching certification. The second meeting is split in two—the first half for learning the rules, and the second half devoted to indoctrinating the coaches in the positive philosophy of NAYS. They watch the NAYS soccer video and then take a quiz based on what they should have learned in their training. A sample of the kind of questions given on the certification exam, used for training both outdoor and indoor soccer coaches, is shown as Exhibit 5.1. As you will note from the questions, the emphasis is on the coach's sensitivity to being a role model to a group of impressionable youngsters. In addition, all coaches must sign the Coaches' Code of Ethics (see Chapter 3). They must also be fingerprinted and cleared by the Ocean City Police Department.

Coaches Certification Exam

1. Kids participate in sports to:
   - ❑ a. Have fun
   - ❑ b. Meet new friends and maintain existing friendships
   - ❑ c. Learn the fundamentals of the game
   - ❑ d. All of the above

2. A positive youth sports experience requires the coach to:
   - ❑ a. Play only the best players
   - ❑ b. Apply pressure to perform
   - ❑ c. Focus only on winning
   - ❑ d. Keep it fun and participatory

3. When planning a practice, the coach should prepare a program that:
   - ❑ a. Focuses on the gifted athletes
   - ❑ b. Separates conditioning from skill development
   - ❑ c. Combines conditioning and skill development
   - ❑ d. None of the above

4. Which of these would NOT be considered child abuse?
   - ❑ a. Slapping a child
   - ❑ b. Using exercise as a punishment
   - ❑ c. Calling children "dumb" when they make mistakes
   - ❑ d. High fives for good plays

5. An athlete should take fluids before, during, and after practice/games.
   - ❑ True   or   ❑ False

6. To prevent accidents at a practice or game, the coach should:
   - ❑ a. Closely supervise the players
   - ❑ b. Assume fields, equipment, and facilities are safe and have been checked
   - ❑ c. Inspect fields, equipment, and facilities for potential hazards every time
   - ❑ d. Both a and c

7. To help prevent injuries:
   - ❑ a. Pit the biggest kids against the smallest
   - ❑ b. Ignore the weather
   - ❑ c. Limit supervision
   - ❑ d. Limit water intake
   - ❑ e. None of the above

8. Positive sports experiences for youth require:
   - ❑ a. Knowledgeable coaches
   - ❑ b. Coordination between coach, parent, and league administrators
   - ❑ c. Doing what is best for the athlete
   - ❑ d. All of the above

9. A good coach will always help every player to:
   - ❑ a. Feel needed
   - ❑ b. Feel a part of the team
   - ❑ c. Feel important
   - ❑ d. All of the above

10. In working with children, which of the following ideas is the most important?
    - ❑ a. Adding stress improves their performance
    - ❑ b. The wide differences of physical and emotional ages for the same chronological age group
    - ❑ c. Exercise for punishment/discipline
    - ❑ d. None of the above

11. A coach who openly argues with an official sends a message to the athletes, parents, and other coaches that this is appropriate behavior in a youth sports setting.
    - ❑ True   or   ❑ False

12. To keep developing my skills and knowledge, so I can be the best youth sports coach I can be, I should:
    - ❑ a. Consult other experienced coaches for tips and advice
    - ❑ b. Ensure that I continue to receive coaching education through publications such as the Youth Sports Journal
    - ❑ c. Review videos and books on coaching
    - ❑ d. All of the above

13. When a coach suspects that a player is the victim of any form of child abuse (emotional, physical, or sexual) he or she is obligated to report it.
    - ❑ True   or   ❑ False

14. Opening lines of communication and developing relationships early can result in parents becoming partners rather than problems.
    - ❑ True   or   ❑ False

15. A youth sports coach should be judged as being effective if:
    - ❑ a. The kids have fun
    - ❑ b. The kids learned something
    - ❑ c. The kids want to continue to participate
    - ❑ d. All of the above

EXHIBIT 5.1   Sample Certification Exam for Coaches

Player Registration and Tryouts

Publicity in the local newspapers announces the dates for player registration and tryouts, with an ample time span between the two for all interested boys and girls to register. For convenience to parents, registration by telephone is available. A child's age, as of August 1 determines which team he or she will play on. For the convenience of all registrants two tryout dates are scheduled one week apart. The tryouts help to assess player skills; they are conducted in small groups and consist of the normal skill sets of dribbling, passing, kicking on goal, and so on. Each player is rated by the coaches on a scale from one to five. Ocean City residents get a two-week advance registration period before others can sign up.

Player Draft

The third coaches meeting takes place after the second tryout and is scheduled for the purpose of drafting the players and assigning them to their respective teams. They use a unique formula that is designed to make the teams as competitively equal as possible. Based on the coaches' cumulative scoring sheets, the eight highest rated players are posted (assuming an eight-team league), then the next best eight, and so forth, for the first four rounds of the draft. This system is designed to balance the teams. Coaches' children are automatically placed on their respective parents' teams. After the fourth round, it is an open draft of the remaining players until all have been assigned to teams. After the draft, the coaches call their respective draftees and inform them of their schedule of practices and games.

A game in the state-of-the-art indoor soccer arena at the Ocean City Recreation Complex. Note the dasher board walls, topped by Plexiglas, and the cushioned tile floor.

This group of five-year-old players in the Tot League hasn't learned position playing yet, but they have plenty of fun bunching up and chasing the ball.

Even in the Tots League an MVP is recognized with a hacky sack for outstanding play.

Indoor soccer has experienced the same type of growth as Little League baseball, with parents wanting to start children younger and younger each year. As might be expected, the Ocean City Rec program for boys and girls, ages four and five, is the most popular, so much so the center has had to limit registration in the past two years. Sure to bring a smile to the faces of all spectators is the way these tots chase the ball up and down the floor with abandon. They are a little young to remember the skills they are taught for any length of time, but there can be little doubt that they're having fun.

Even at this early age, the youngsters thrive on a taste of the recognition of achievement—whether they win or not. In their competitive games, a Most Valuable Player is chosen, based on his or her effort. This MVP receives a token award, such as a hacky-sack miniature soccer ball with his or her name put on it in magic marker.

These young children will of course feed systematically into the older age-groups. Indoor soccer leagues are organized in ages from 6 to 26. Youth leagues include U8, U10, U12, U14, and U16, with U meaning *under*. (U10 would be under age 10 but older than 8, when the next age-group begins.) These leagues are recreational and are scheduled on Saturdays.

The indoor soccer season is three months long, from December through February. Tryouts, the player draft, and team practices are scheduled in November. A typical schedule, this one for the Indoor Soccer U10 Division, is shown as Exhibit 5.2.

Soccer-Rama

A popular end-of-the-season tournament, called Soccer-Rama, is scheduled on the last Saturday of the season. It is designed as a fun last event of the season, followed by a big party. There are no losers; every team plays every other team in successive round-robin games of 15 minutes. It is fast moving and everyone has fun. At the end of Soccer-Rama, the teams have a big party in the center's community room, and trophies are presented to the players of *every* participating team. This reinforces the philosophy of encouraging youngsters to play their best and have fun, win or lose.

Competitive indoor soccer leagues play on Sunday for U12 and older children. The Sunday Competitive League is designed for travel teams that play around the state. There are also tournaments, the largest being the annual Saint Patrick's Weekend Tournament in March. Forty-eight teams from Maryland, Pennsylvania, and Delaware come to play in an elimination tournament. It is for teams in the U10 through U16 age ranges.

The Ocean City Recreation and Parks Department sponsors a Winterfest Soccer Camp over the Christmas holidays. Kevin Darcy, a former professional soccer player and current coach at Salisbury School, conducts

Indoor Soccer U10 Division

12/08/01

			Time	Location
O.C. Berlin Optimist/Klienstuber	vs.	O.C. Rec. Boosters/Danaher	9:00 A.M.	east gym
Planet Maze/Thaler	vs.	Coates, Coates, & Coates/Gray	10:00 A.M.	east gym
Greene Turtle/Dickerson	vs.	Bull on the Beach/Mitchell	11:00 A.M.	east gym
Phillips Crabhouse/Meekins	vs.	Marlins/Forte	noon	east gym

12/15/01

			Time	Location
Planet Maze/Thaler	vs.	Marlins/Forte	9:00 A.M.	east gym
Greene Turtle/Dickerson	vs.	Phillips Crabhouse/Meekins	10:00 A.M.	east gym
O.C. Rec. Boosters/Danaher	vs.	Bull on the Beach/Mitchell	11:00 A.M.	east gym
Coates, Coates, & Coates/Gray	vs.	O.C. Berlin Optimist/Klienstuber	noon	east gym

01/05/02

			Time	Location
O.C. Berlin Optimist/Klienstuber	vs.	Bull on the Beach/Mitchell	9:00 A.M.	east gym
Coates, Coates, & Coates/Gray	vs.	Marlins/Forte	10:00 A.M.	east gym
O.C. Rec. Boosters/Danaher	vs.	Phillips Crabhouse/Meekins	11:00 A.M.	east gym
Planet Maze/Thaler	vs.	Greene Turtle/Dickerson	noon	east gym

01/12/02

			Time	Location
O.C. Rec. Boosters/Danaher	vs.	Planet Maze/Thaler	9:00 A.M.	east gym
Marlins/Forte	vs.	O.C. Berlin Optimist/Klienstuber	10:00 A.M.	east gym
Coates, Coates, & Coates/Gray	vs.	Greene Turtle/Dickerson	11:00 A.M.	east gym
Bull on the Beach/Mitchell	vs.	Phillips Crabhouse/Meekins	noon	east gym

01/19/02

			Time	Location
Marlins/Forte	vs.	Greene Turtle/Dickerson	9:00 A.M.	east gym
O.C. Berlin Optimist/Klienstuber	vs.	Phillips Crabhouse/Meekins	10:00 A.M.	east gym
Bull on the Beach/Mitchell	vs.	Planet Maze/Thaler	11:00 A.M.	east gym
Coates, Coates, & Coates/Gray	vs.	O.C. Rec. Boosters/Danaher	noon	east gym

02/02/02

			Time	Location
Bull on the Beach/Mitchell	vs.	Coates, Coates, & Coates/Gray	9:00 A.M.	east gym
Marlins/Forte	vs.	O.C. Rec. Boosters/Danaher	10:00 A.M.	east gym
Phillips Crabhouse/Meekins	vs.	Planet Maze/Thaler	11:00 A.M.	east gym
Greene Turtle/Dickerson	vs.	O.C. Berlin Optimist/Klienstuber	noon	east gym

02/09/02

			Time	Location
Greene Turtle/Dickerson	vs.	O.C. Rec. Boosters/Danaher	9:00 A.M.	east gym
O.C. Berlin Optimist/Klienstuber	vs.	Planet Maze/Thaler	10:00 A.M.	east gym
Phillips Crabhouse/Meekins	vs.	Coates, Coates, & Coates/Gray	11:00 A.M.	east gym
Marlins/Forte	vs.	Bull on the Beach/Mitchell	noon	east gym

SINGLE ELIMINATION PLAYOFF BEGINS 02/16/02.

EXHIBIT 5.2   Indoor Soccer U10 Division schedule

it. There is a three-day camp from 10:00 A.M. to 3:00 P.M. for boys and girls ages 6 to 16.

In the indoor soccer leagues, Ocean City Rec's philosophy is "everybody plays," that is, every attempt is made to provide equal playing time to every roster player. Individual skill development is encouraged, and "playing hard to win" is stressed over winning itself.

Keep It Simple, Make It Fun

This is the underlying philosophy of the youth soccer program. "Everybody plays" is the rule, and every attempt must be made to provide equal playing time to every player. This is probably easier to achieve in indoor soccer than in most other youth sports because the intensity of play and minimum number of time-outs require frequent substitutions. In Chapter 4, we mentioned that in outdoor soccer, with 11 players on a team, there are games in which one or more players never touch the ball. That will never

Members of a U12 team celebrate and raise their trophies after the completion of Soccer-Rama.

happen in indoor soccer due to the fact that there are fewer players in a more confined field of play. Every player gets involved, and every player welcomes an occasional rest period.

Consistent with having coaches sign a Coaches' Code of Ethics, parents are also asked to show their commitment by signing a copy of the Parent's Code of Ethics. It is shown in Chapter 11, "Dealing with Parents and Pressure."

CHAPTER 6

Skills, Drills, and Games for Youth Soccer Practice

You may have heard the old story about the young violinist who stopped a stranger in New York City and asked, "How do you get to Carnegie Hall?" The punch line was, "Practice, practice, practice." If a young soccer player asked, "How do you get to the World Cup," the answer would be the same. There is nothing that correlates better to number of team wins than the number of practices. That doesn't mean we are fostering a winning-is-every-thing philosophy. It just means we recognize two basic facts: more practices equal more wins, and winning is more fun than losing. A coach that mini-mizes practices between games will usually develop a team that loses more games than it wins. Losing consistently isn't fun, and the coach will begin to suffer some of the by-product symptoms of a losing season: players not showing up for games, loss of self esteem among players, grumpy parents, and so on. Our recommended goal to a new coach is to plan for a winning season—more wins than losses—by instilling in his team the importance of practice, practice, practice. That doesn't mean just team practice, but a combination of team and individual practice. Remind your players, on an individual basis, that the more shots on goal they practice, the more goals they will make. It's a mathematical certainty!

In Chapter 12, "Winning," we give you a formula that is sure to produce a winning season for your team. The first step in that formula is to practice every day—not necessarily team practice every day, but at least a combination of team and individual practice. Football coaches at one time made halfbacks who were prone to fumbling carry a football everywhere they went. Maybe giving your players a soccer ball, or even a hacky sack, would keep them focused on the individual skills that will make them better players.

From the 1950s till the 1980s, one could drive through any neighbor-hood and see boys and girls playing baseball in the streets, the parks, and even their yards, just having a catch with a friend. Take that same drive today and you'll see kids doing the same thing, but with a soccer ball. Kids in Europe have been doing it for years, and finally it has caught on in America, where kids practice, practice, practice.

There are few sports in which the fundamentals can be broken down into so few basic skills as soccer: passing, receiving, kicking, heading, trapping, controlling, goalkeeping—if you know these, you know them all. And there are probably few other athletic skills that can show the results of practice, practice, practice more quickly than in soccer. We're not just talking team practice, but also home practice—with dad or a friend, or individual practice bouncing the ball against a wall. All of what we have said would apply equally to outdoor and indoor soccer. But when you add a wall to the scenario, you increase the versatility of the player, speed up the game, and make it more fun.

Ask a sweating 300-pound lineman at professional football camp if he enjoys practice, and he would be lying if he said yes. Whether it's football, baseball, or piano lessons, the usual reaction to the word *practice* is "Yuck!"

So you as a youth soccer coach have a real challenge to make your soccer practice fun. It can be done with equal measures of imagination and motivation. That's why we throw games into the equation. Kids like games, so if you break down your practice sessions into skill and drill games, they become fun instead of drudgery. Throw in a few incentives to challenge them to break the standing record or their own personal record. Or simply reward them with inexpensive surprises, such as bubble gum, candy, or game cards for achieving something that is exceptional *for the individual*. Maybe it is a hacky sack, or a water bottle or a wristband or headband in the team colors. Check out your local cheap novelty store and you will find some interesting items.

There are so many possible skills/drills/games that it will require two chapters to explain and illustrate them. As outlined in the Introduction, this chapter will include generic skills, drills, and games that can apply to either outdoor or indoor soccer. Chapter 7 will relate to indoor soccer only. Both sets of drills can be changed or altered, depending on the age group you are coaching. Keep in mind that the objective is to make them fun. During drills, remind your players that possession means goals, goals mean wins, and winning is fun.

Warming Up and Stretching

No matter what the sport, or the age of the participant, no player should go on the playing field without warming up and stretching. A pitcher in baseball is not ready to pitch unless he has broken a sweat during warm-ups. One of the problems in the coach-parent relationship occurs when parents don't bring their children to the field in time to warm up. How many times have you, as a coach, scanned the entrance to the field, looking for a key player who hasn't arrived? And how many times has the player jumped out of the car, a minute before the game is to start and run on the field without a warm-up? The player is neither mentally nor physically ready, and the lack of a warm-up and stretching regime is an invitation to injury.

We are grateful to Brian Quinn and Ralf Wilhelms, professional indoor soccer players, coaches, and authors of the instructional CD-ROM *Learn to Play and Coach Indoor Soccer*, for allowing us to use the warm-up/stretching exercises they recommend for indoor soccer players at all levels. They cover all of the parts of the body that are actively used in soccer:

- Lower Back: Spread feet far enough apart so your palms can touch the ground when you bend at the waist. Keep your knees straight. This is a general stretch for hamstring and back extendors.
- Hamstring: In a sitting position, spread your legs. Keep the knee of the leg to be stretched straight. Lean forward and reach for the sole of that foot. Repeat with other leg. Feel the stretch in your back, behind your knee, and your thigh.
- Hip-flexor: Assume a half-kneeling position. Tighten your stomach muscles and keep your back straight. Push your hip forward to feel the stretch in the top of your thigh.
- Calves: Stand, leaning against a wall, with the leg to be stretched behind you, and the other leg bent in front of you. Point toes forward, not to the side. Lean your body forward and down until you feel the stretching in the calf of the straight leg. Don't allow your heel to lift up. Repeat with other leg.
- Quadriceps: Stand, holding onto a support with one hand. Bend one knee and take hold of the ankle. Do not lock the knee of the leg you are standing on. Draw your heel toward your buttock. Tilt your hip forward so that your knee points toward the floor. Repeat with the other leg.
- Lower Back: Lie on your back. Pull your knees toward your chest. Roll along the spine.
- Back: Start on your knees with hands on the floor and trunk rounded like a cat. Slowly lower your chest toward the floor, arching your back. In one fluid motion, extend your hips, trunk, and neck.
- Trapezius: Stand or sit. Bring the arm you want to stretch behind your neck. Grasp your wrist with other hand and pull as far as possible toward the opposite shoulder. Side bend the trunk slightly away from the arm being stretched. You should feel the stretch in the side of your trunk and shoulder. Repeat with the other arm.
- Groin: Sit on floor with soles of your feet together as close to your groin as possible. Push your knees toward the floor. Stretch the inside of your thighs.

If the coach has enough soccer balls for every player, there are some individual warm-up exercises players can do on their own:

- Stand to the side of a ball. With feet together, jump laterally back and forth over the ball; then forward and backward.
- Stand with legs straddled, holding a ball overhead with arms extended. In sequence, to a count, touch the ball to the ground next to the left foot; return the ball overhead, then touch the ball to the ground next to the right foot, etc.
- Sit on the ground with legs outstretched. Roll the ball along the ground around the back, around the outstretched legs, and continuing around your back again.
- Lie flat on the ground on your back with legs straight and arms stretched out on the ground above your head. Place a ball between your feet and lift it up to place it in your hands. Bring your feet back to the ground, and return the ball between the feet to repeat the exercise.

These are individual exercises; once you have taught them and explained their importance, players can go through the exercises on their own. Have some pregame drills ready to start as soon as your first player finishes the stretching exercises. Make them active drills involving running, so the kids will work up a sweat before the game starts. If nothing else, have them run laps. If you as coach aren't prepared with drills, your players will start their own disorganized pregame play, which may not utilize the pregame time constructively.

Basic Skills

The following are the basic individual skills a coach should teach and every player should master.

Dribbling

The skill of dribbling involves learning to touch the ball with any part of the foot, while moving forward, backward, or to the side and keeping control of the ball at all times. A player should learn to change feet, speed, and direction while dribbling. Dribbling is a skill that can be practiced anywhere, with or without another player. It can be set up as a relay drill in group practice, with teams on either end of the floor. Teach young players to stay on their toes to make it possible to adjust their position to the ball at any time. It is important to keep control of the ball and be ready to change directions quickly when challenged. It is also important for dribblers to keep their head up at all times. The floor of the indoor soccer court is even,

Relay team dribbling will improve this skill and add an element of competition to make it more fun.

so the sole of the foot becomes the control stick for changing direction and speed of the dribble.

The player who can dribble well, keep control of the ball, and fake out an opponent with a variety of creative sleight-of-foot moves is the player who takes soccer seriously, has fun, and practices, practices, practices. Perhaps because soccer has been the national sport in most European countries (whereas it is baseball in America), the youngsters there grow up using their feet, not their hands, in manipulating a ball. Because of that difference, we coaches should invoke the no-hands rule in practice, as in a game, to teach the inexperienced player not to touch the ball with his or her hands at any time.

Shielding or Covering

This is dribbling against a defensive player. A good dribbler must learn how to cover the ball, and keep it away from the opposition. The dribbler must not turn his or her back on the opponent. Doing so makes it too easy for the ball to be stolen, either from around the legs or through them. When the dribbler turns his back on a defender, the dribbler can't see the defender or the rest of the opposing team. The correct way to cover-up or shield is a sideways turn or dribble, which gives the player a wider stance and shields the ball from the defense. Players must learn to keep the body between the ball and the opposing player at all times. A soccer player who also plays basketball will recognize the same strategy in both sports.

This player is starting to execute a sideward turn to shield against the opponent closing in on her left.

Passing

The kicking foot should be sideways to the ball, with a locked ankle. The ball should be hit close to the middle of the foot, with the ball hit in the center. The kicking foot should continue the swing through, with the other foot pointed in the direction you want the ball to travel. Most young players use this method for passing, but it's important to remind them that passing can also mean heading or pushing the ball to a teammate, using any part of the body but the hands. Push-passing the ball among your teammates allows the team to maintain control of the ball until someone sees an opportunity to take a shot on goal.

Pro soccer coaches say if you can't pass, you shouldn't be playing soccer. In youth soccer that may be true of the experienced player, but for the beginner it is the skill that usually requires the greatest amount of practice. Passing has a lot to do with teammates and space. It is like a quarterback in football who doesn't pass to his receiver; he passes to the space where his receiver will be when the ball arrives. The beginner will pass to a player; the experienced player will pass to a space the teammate is moving toward. This skill develops teamwork more than any other. It requires studying your teammate and learning to sense the next move—just as quarterbacks do with their receivers. Young players should know where the pass is supposed to go before the ball hits the instep.

A good passing drill for one player is to pass off the board, picking a spot on the board as the target, let the ball come back through the legs toward the other side of the arena, then control it and pass it to the board on the other side. Keep doing this, back and forth across the arena. It is a good drill for both controlling the ball and improving passing accuracy.

The girl on the right is passing the ball with her kicking foot sideways to the ball and with a locked ankle.

Ball Control

In baseball, if a team can hit but can't catch, you have the potential of a hard-hitting losing team. In soccer, if your players can dribble and pass but can't receive and control, you may have the same result—a losing season, which is not fun.

Again the analogy is football, the relationship between the quarterback and the receiver. The quarterback may throw a perfect pass, the receiver may get his hands on it, but if he can't control it, the pass is not complete. It is the same in a soccer pass; if a player passes to a spot, and the teammate reaches that spot, as planned, that is good execution on the part of both players. But it's not enough for the receiving player to be in the right place at the right time, if the player can't control the ball after receiving it. The player receiving the ball must get in front of the ball as it comes to him, but must also be aware of the surroundings to get prepared for what he is going to do with the ball. Players must learn ball control, as ball possession and offensive control are what results in outscoring the other team. In professional football you hear the announcers commenting on "time of possession," and usually the team that wins in that category also wins the game. The same is true of indoor soccer. The team that controls the ball more—or keeps the ball in its scoring half of the field longer—is nearly always the winning team. Controlling the ball means being alert to where the ball was, is, and will be, as well as knowing what you're going to do with the ball. The expression "playing heads-up ball" is particularly true of the indoor soccer player, because the pace of the game is so fast. You can spot a good player by the position of his or her head while dribbling. It is the same in basketball, where the playmaking guard is busy looking for the spot to pass the ball to a teammate heading for that spot. A good player in both sports has what we call a sense of the playing field. This player knows where he or she is in relation to the other players on the field at all times.

In the photograph below the player is not looking down at the ball, he's looking up, surveying where his teammates are and where the open spaces are. Without control, soccer would be like golf: a process of hitting the ball and chasing it. We expect the five- and six-year-olds to spend most of their time bunching up and chasing the ball. Their well-coached older siblings hold their positions, control the ball, and keep possession of it, staying on offense as much as possible.

The player controls the ball with his foot as he looks for open space to pass.

Trapping

Players must learn to trap the ball with any part of their body, excluding the hands. They must, at the very least, not let a pass get by them. Juggling is a good one-player ball-control drill—you keep the ball in your possession, alternately using head, chest, knee, and foot to control it. A good one-player drill is to toss the ball against the wall, trap it on the chest, juggle it off the thigh (or knee), and catch it on the instep. Another one-player drill is to juggle the ball, first with a bounce, then without a bounce, and finally, while seated, juggle it with the foot. It's a drill that can be practiced anywhere. All you need is a ball and a player who wants to practice. In a game situation, the player must be aggressive and move to the ball to control it, not wait for the ball to come to her. Once she reaches the ball, the savvy player will get and maintain control of it, using her body to shield the ball so the defensive player doesn't steal it.

Heading

This is one of the hardest skills to learn, not only in terms of *how* to use the head, but also in terms of *when* to head the ball. Young players must learn to keep their eyes open when heading. They must learn to use their forehead, not the top of their head. That requires being able to judge the height and speed of the ball, and being able to aim the forehead so the ball connects with it at the right time. The experienced player will learn, with practice, how to direct the ball toward a selected target. A volleyball can be used to teach younger players about the skill of heading.

There have been many studies on the adverse effect of heading on young players, so although it is a skill that should be practiced, it should not be overdone. Be aware of possible fallout from parents who may have read about these studies. Improper heading is not healthy at any age. Limit the repetition of the heading drills and the length of practice time.

A good way to teach and practice heading with the U10, U8, and Tots leagues is to use a soft sponge ball, or Nerf ball, gradually working up to a soccer ball. You can also use a large red kickball, which is softer than a regulation soccer ball.

Practice is the key, and it can be done alone at home, heading the ball against a wall or garage door, or with someone else, taking turns throwing the ball at various heights and angles to force the player to move to the ball and head it toward a specific target.

Using his knee and chest, this player traps the ball to bring it under control.

The coach conducts a heading drill by throwing the ball in the air, as the player aims his forehead to head it back.

Shooting

You won't have any trouble persuading your players to practice this skill—that's because it's fun! Point out to them that soccer has produced some of the best field goal kickers in professional football. They have learned these basics of the soccer kick:

1. Keep the ankle locked.
2. Keep the head down (same as baseball and golf).
3. Keep the toe down.
4. Hit the ball dead center.
5. Kick with the instep to maximize power.
6. Follow through.
7. Learn to shoot with both feet.

An essential aspect of shooting is the importance of the plant foot. The plant foot refers to whichever foot will not be striking the ball for the shot. The placement and angle of the plant foot determine the direction and strength of the shot. The proper technique is to place the plant foot directly parallel to the ball, pointing in the direction in which the shot is intended to travel. Placing the plant foot alongside the ball in this manner guarantees that the shooter will have his or her weight properly balanced leading into the shot, which is critical for strength as well as accuracy. Also, whichever direction the toe of the plant foot is facing is the same direction the shooter's shot will follow.

The player's foot is positioned properly, with the instep ready to kick the ball.

More shots mean more goals; more goals mean more wins. Making more accurate shots on goal means more practice, practice, practice.

Wherever possible on skill drills, set up records of each player's scores to measure improvement; for example, number of goals versus attempts in a shoot-on-goal drill. The pat on the back you give a player who has improved his or her score is worth its weight in smiles. Cone dribbling is another example of such a drill, since the player's time in dribbling through all of the cones can be recorded with a stopwatch.

A fun drill to practice shooting is to place a ball about 10 to 12 feet away from the goal, directly in front of it. Place a young player next to the ball, but looking away from goal toward the opposite goal. On your call, have the player turn around quickly, and in one movement kick the ball on goal. It is a good drill to measure a player's *feel* for the net, when he or she doesn't see it until the last moment. Some coaches call it smelling the goal.

Key
G = goalie
X = offensive player
H-O-R-S-E = kicking locations

Drills and Games

Here are some drills and games we recommend you use in practice:

Horse

The objective is to score on a goalie from five different locations. Each player kicks from all sides, taking the five stations that spell out H-O-R-S-E, as shown in Exhibit 6.1.

Left corner with left foot (H)

Left angle with left foot (O)

Direct kick with dominant foot (R)

Right angle with right foot (S)

Right side with right foot (E)

It is excellent practice for kicks on goal; especially good for taking advantage of situations where there is no opposition—that is, where the goalie has been pulled away from the mouth of the goal. These are scoring opportunities that should always result in a score. The player who misses the easy one will pay more attention in your next practice to the shoot-on-goal drill. An overanxious player, or one who tries to shoot

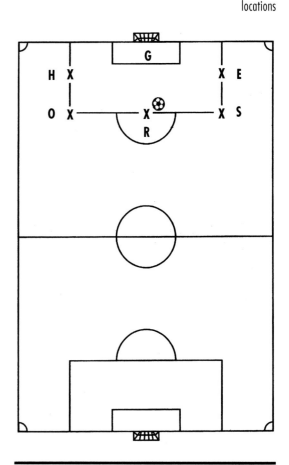

EXHIBIT 6.1   H-O-R-S-E Drill

In the drill for H-O-R-S-E, five players form a semicircle facing the goalie and rotate after each trial kick. In a game version, the winner is the first who can score from each of the five positions.

while off-balance, may fail to capitalize on this rare opportunity and miss the goal. Repetitive drills are the answer to making this play routine.

Cone Dribbling

This is a drill that can be used in either indoor or outdoor soccer. The objective is to wind in and around cones, while keeping control of the ball. The overanxious player will kick the ball too hard, or inaccurately, and end up in a frustrating attempt to regain control and/or proper position. The emphasis of this drill must be on ball control, not speed. See Exhibit 6.2.

The coach should use a stopwatch to measure the elapsed time from the beginning to the end of the drill, but keeping control of the ball is just as important as speed in dribbling the ball. If a player loses control of the

Key   △ = offense   ---- = ball and player/path

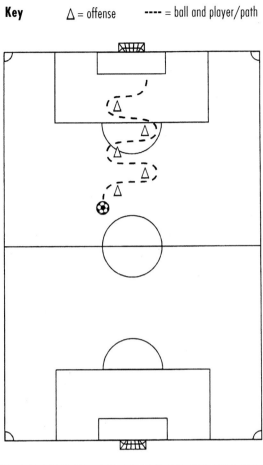

EXHIBIT 6.2   Cone Dribbling Drill

Each player dribbles through the cone maze, keeping control of the ball, while the coach checks the time with a stopwatch.

ball, he or she must repeat the drill. It should demonstrate to the players, in comparing times, that the player who controls the ball best will also be the player who has the best time. This should discourage players who get over-anxious in their dribbling, and it should encourage patience and accuracy in the skill of dribbling. To add a little more action to this drill, have the cones run toward the goal, and add a goalie to guard the net. As the players run the cone drill, have them take a shot at the goal as they come around a cone and see an opening.

Key   **O** = team A   ⟵ = movement of player
X = team B

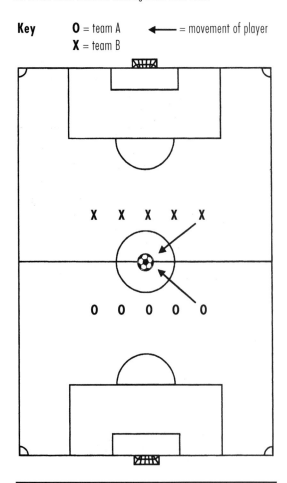

EXHIBIT 6.3   Steal the Bacon Game

Steal the Bacon

Exhibit 6.3 shows a variation of an old children's game. The players are equally divided into two teams. The players are numbered, with each team having the same numbers; if there are five on a team, each team has a number 1, a number 2, and so on. The ball is placed in the middle. The coach calls out a number, and the two opposing players with that number run to the ball. The object is to see who can get to the ball first and kick it toward the other team. It provides good one-on-one competition. To add a little more action in the drill, the coach can call two numbers, which results in four players competing for "the bacon."

Like-numbered members of two teams compete to reach and control the ball first.

Circle Passing

The team makes a circle in the center of the
practice area. The coach calls the direction,
either left or right, for the player with the ball to
pass. The player currently with the ball must
listen to the coach's call and be able to change
direction when the call is made. This drill
teaches the players to gain control of the ball
quickly and move it on to a teammate before a
defending player moves in, as shown in Exhibit
6.4. To make this drill more competitive, play it
like musical chairs; the player who passes the
ball in the wrong direction, or misplays a pass, is
out. Play until there is only one player left: the
winner!

Controlling the ball is very important in
soccer, and even more important in indoor
soccer. As a fun variation of the circle passing
drill, you can play the game of odd man out.
When a player bobbles the pass, or doesn't trap,
that player is removed from the circle. You
continue the drill until there are only two players
left. Keep reminding your players that as long as
your team has the ball, the other team can't
score.

Key O = player   ↻ = change ball direction
---- = ball path

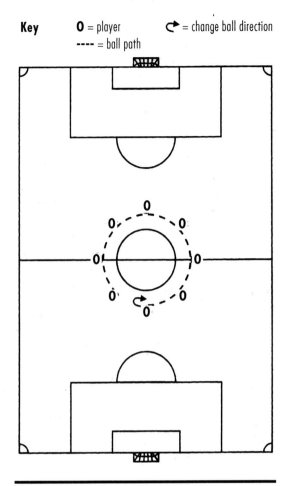

EXHIBIT 6.4   Circle Passing Drill

On command, players pass
the ball to left or right
around the circle. When a
player fails to control the
ball, he or she drops out.

Key   **X** = first player and   **O** = second player
ball direction   copying first player

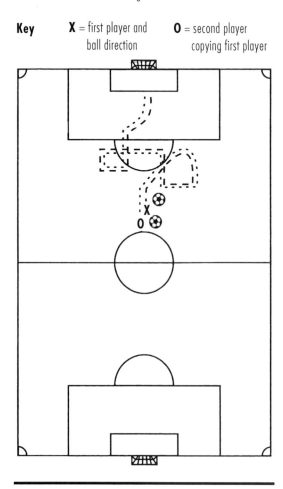

EXHIBIT 6.5 Copycat Dribbling Drill

Copycat Dribbling

Two players, each with a ball, line up, one behind the other. The lead player makes different moves with the ball, as he or she pushes forward. The second player must copy the first, using his or her own ball. For example, if the first player dribbles right, the second player dribbles right; if the first dribbles in a circle, the second does the same; if the first bounces the ball off the wall, the second repeats the maneuver. This is a great drill to practice "possession." See Exhibit 6.5.

Remind your players that the team that keeps control of the ball, and continues to be on the offensive, is most likely going to be the winning team. Learning to dribble and use the wall as a teammate is important to indoor soccer. Dribbling involves a lot of technique, and the clever ball handler can create his own repertoire of moves to fake the defender out of position and prevent him from stealing the ball. Your best ball handlers will enjoy this drill, because it gives them a chance to showcase their dribbling skills, while teaching the other players those skills. They will enjoy the exciting experience of dribbling past the other team's defense and moving in on goal to make a shot.

Your best dribblers execute various dribbling maneuvers for the less experienced players to follow.

In scheduling the sequence of the drills, the coach should be alert to signs that the players are getting tired of one drill and quickly change to another. You will soon recognize which are the drills the kids consider the most fun and change to those drills when you sense they are getting bored.

For practice before a game, you should always have one or two drills ready to use. Keep your team organized and utilize active drills to help the players get warmed up for the game.

CHAPTER 7

Off-the-Wall Drills for Indoor Youth Soccer Practice

In the previous chapter we covered basic skills applicable to both indoor and outdoor soccer. This chapter will add a wall, a shorter field of play, and a much faster pace of play for your players who are experienced in outdoor soccer. You will recognize the players on your team who have played outdoor soccer. Presumably they should be the easiest to teach the basics of indoor soccer. However, some of them may have developed lazy habits in the less demanding game of outdoor soccer, so you will have the challenge of teaching them to stay focused for the speed and endurance required in indoor soccer. If you are a new coach who may have coached outdoor soccer, you will immediately see the difference between the indoor and outdoor sports.

Coaching soccer really means teaching and development, but recreational and competitive soccer is *not* school, and the kids want to have fun. They will have had their fill of school before they come to practice. A good coach needs to keep that in mind. Winning is important, and more fun than losing, but watching young players develop and have fun is more important. Many of the drills discussed in this chapter can be altered, depending on the age group, keeping in mind the objective is fun. We have designed them, for the sake of this book, for youth soccer. During drills, remind your players that possession means goals, goals mean wins, and winning is fun.

A drill is what the name implies: constant repetition until the skill becomes instinctive. We coaches have the opportunity to teach impressionable youngsters skills they can use all their lives. Because they are impressionable—and eager to learn—they will accept the repetitive nature of the drill and savor the satisfaction of using it successfully in a game. But the learning curve will improve dramatically when the coach makes the drill fun. Then it becomes a game within itself, and practice will become enjoyable and not boring. You'll know you have made it as a coach when you walk into the arena for practice and see a few of your players already out on the floor practicing a drill you taught them a week or two ago.

In Chapter 6 we presented skills, drills, and games for youth soccer practice. They were generic drills, equally applicable in their use to either outdoor or indoor soccer. In this chapter we are presenting off-the-wall drills that are designed specifically for indoor soccer. Here are some drills we have used successfully.

Practice time is sometimes at a premium in indoor soccer arenas, so the savvy coach will seek other hard, flat surfaces for practice. School gymnasiums, basketball courts, and parking lots that are not in use can work just fine for the generic drills shown in Chapter 6. Essentially you will be practicing *futsal*, which is played without dasher boards.

Wherever possible, keep a record of each player's scores to measure improvement during drills. The pat on the back you give when you tell a player he has improved his score will make his day. Cone dribbling (Chapter 6) is an example of such a drill—the player's time in dribbling through all of the cones can be recorded with a stopwatch. Speed passing is another drill in which a stopwatch can be used to measure how many passes can be completed within a given time period. When you get the use of an arena for practice, there are a number of off-the-wall team drills we would recommend you use in practice. You will notice the first several are drills for shooting on goal. These will be your most popular drills. Watch your players who arrive early for practice, and go out on the floor. Do they practice dribbling or passing or heading or dribbling? No way. They will start taking practice kicks on goal but in a disorganized way. We recommend you instill an early-to-practice routine. The first thing they should do is go through the nine stretching exercises outlined at the beginning of Chapter 6. Then give a ball to each of the first pairs who finish their warm-up routine and have them go through this two-player practice:

1. First player starts at the red line, touches the ball once, then shoots it on goal.
2. Second player does the same.
3. First player starts at the red line, passes ball off the boards, and then shoots it on goal when it rebounds.
4. Second player does the same.
5. First player passes the ball to second who passes it off the boards, and first player shoots the rebound on goal.
6. Players reverse roles on drill 5.

As additional players drift in, pair them off with a ball to follow the same drill. If you can discipline your team to automatically go into this regime as they arrive at the arena, you will have them focusing on playing soccer rather than horsing around prior to a game. A lot of unnecessary injuries occur when unsupervised players are horsing around.

Following are the team off-the-wall drills.

Off-the-Back-Wall Rebound Scoring

Obviously this is one that is totally indoor soccer–oriented. The coach throws (or kicks) the ball against the wall behind the goal, so it will bounce back toward a charging offensive player. The coach should change his position from the left side to the right, so the player will be charging the ball from various angles. The objective is for the player to gain control of the bouncing ball and take a shot on goal. Be sure to include the "weak foot" in the drill, the left foot of a right-footed player and vice versa. It is a great strength-builder for the weaker foot, and great practice for game situations.

Key
C = coach
O = offense
---- = ball path

Make the player control the ball so he can kick the goal with the predominant foot. In assessing the strengths of your players take note of those who are left-footed so you can position them on the left facing the goal. Left-footed kickers, especially *good* left-footed kickers are rare. Finding a good southfoot to play left wing will be a real bonus for your team.

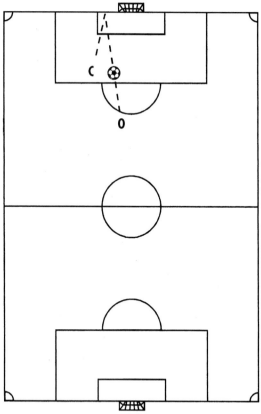

EXHIBIT 7.1   Off-the-Back-Wall Rebound Scoring Drill

This shows the sequence of the coach, starting to the left of the goal, throwing the ball against the back wall (1), the ball bouncing off the wall (2), and the player catching the ball on the rebound and kicking it on goal (3).

Off-the-Wall Corner Drill

This is similar to the previous drill. An offensive player is moving toward the goal, first from the left, then from the right side. The coach throws or kicks a ball against the side dasher board so that it ricochets to the center toward the goal. The player quickly gains control of the ball and takes a shot on goal. Use the drill both with and without a goalie defending. As a variation, have a player, instead of the coach, oversee this exercise. It will give him or her good experience in developing a feel for where the ball goes off the corner dasher boards. (See Exhibit 7.2.)

Off-the-Wall Passing

This is a two-player drill designed to help players learn how to play the angles and pass-ricochet the ball to teammates, as they are coming down the floor parallel to the side wall. It should be practiced from the left and then from the right. The first player dribbles the ball along the sideboard, watching a teammate in the center. With appropriate timing, she kicks the ball at an angle so that it bounces off the side wall and rebounds to the teammate. Keeping control of the ball throughout this drill is very important. (See Exhibit 7.3.)

This can be practiced by two teammates, without an opponent, but it's more fun, and more realistic, when you insert a defensive player who tries to keep the first player from making the rebound pass. This is also a good defensive drill.

Off-the-Wall Target Practice

Near the offensive goal, a large X is placed on the side board as a kicking target. Players line up and take turns kicking at target X. The drill is repeated at varying distances and angles. The object of the drill is for the players to see where the ball rebounds, with respect to the goal, depending on distance, angle, and velocity of the kick. You will never have problems getting your team to participate in this drill, as it involves some of their favorite aspects of the sport: kicking and targets.

When the players get good at this, try it again, and let each player call where he or she wants a teammate to intercept the ball and take a shot on goal.

Key   **O** = offense   ---- = ball path

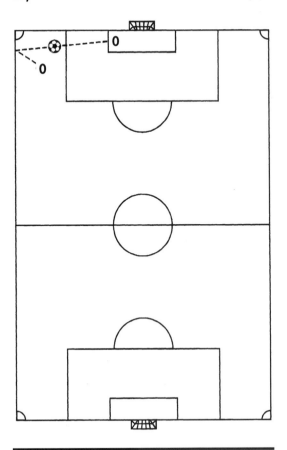

EXHIBIT 7.2   Off-the-Wall Corner Drill

Key   **O** = offense   ---- = ball path
           X = defense

EXHIBIT 7.3   Off-the-Wall Pass Using the Wall as a Teammate

As the opponent in the center moves toward the girl with the ball, she prepares to kick the ball against the wall so it will ricochet to her teammate on the left.

In off-the-wall target practice the X target is clearly visible to the player taking the shot, while another player waits her turn.

Off-the-Wall Drills for One or Two Players

The newest game played with a soccer ball is SocCourt, which was described at the end of Chapter 2. It is a cross between soccer and handball (without the hands). As a one-player drill, it resembles what young players of various sports have been doing for years; i.e., bouncing a ball against a wall or steps and playing it off the bounce. Your players may have done it at home, bouncing a rubber ball or tennis ball off a wall or steps. However, in those instances they have used their hands to catch the ball off the bounce. In a soccer drill, however, they can't use their hands, so the players must play the ball off other parts of the body: foot, chest, head, etc.

It can be made a one-player game by players keeping track of how many bounces they can make against the wall and keep the ball in play. Encourage them to keep track of their best score and then try to beat it. The two-player drill/game version is started by the server throwing the ball against the wall (the only time the hands are used). The other player must play the ball off the wall, using a part of his body other than hands, and return the ball against the wall. Unlike handball, two bounces are allowed. Hence the receiver could trap the ball with the chest, or head the ball, so that on the second bounce it would be positioned for a hard kick against the wall. Like the scoring in volleyball, points are scored only when a player serves the ball. You can either give each player five serves, as in ping-pong,

Two players, a ball, and a wall are all you need to have a game of SocCourt, a combination of soccer and handball (without the hands of course).

alternating the serve, or change serves every time a server loses possession of the ball. This is a great competitive drill. It's designed to sharpen a player's ability to control the ball, either by trapping, heading, or controlling it with the foot, and improve scoring accuracy after gaining control of the ball. And it's a drill that a player can do at home, as well as in team practice, just by bouncing the soccer ball against a wall and controlling the rebound.

Short Passing

The objective is to practice the short-passing skills that are required in indoor soccer. The close-up, precise pass is a necessity in indoor soccer, due to the size of the playing field. Players are set up in a triangle about 10 to 15 feet apart. Players must pass to the next player to the inside of a teammate's foot, so the player can stop the ball, gain control, and then pass it on to the next teammate. As an added fun drill, set up teams of three players in a triangle, and see which team gets in the most passes within a set time period. Deduct a point whenever the ball leaves the circle.

Speed Passing

Speed passing is important because in indoor soccer the defensive players are so much closer to the offense. This drill takes dribbling and passing to a new level of speed. The speed-passing drill is set up the same as for short-passing, but the players must complete the drill three times within two

In the short-passing drill three players are in a triangle, the one on the right using his instep to make a short, accurate pass to his waiting teammate.

For the long-passing drill the triangle is expanded, so the distance between players is greater, which requires harder, faster passes that can't be intercepted.

minutes. As in the short-passing drill, deduct a point if the ball leaves the circle, or a player loses control of the ball.

To make it fun, set up teams of three players each and have the teams compete to achieve the best time. As an added drill, have each team move toward the goal while kicking the ball back and forth. This puts the drill in a game situation, reinforcing the strategy of always moving toward the goal, while making the drill more like a game.

Key   **O** = offense   ← = movement of player
          ---- = ball path

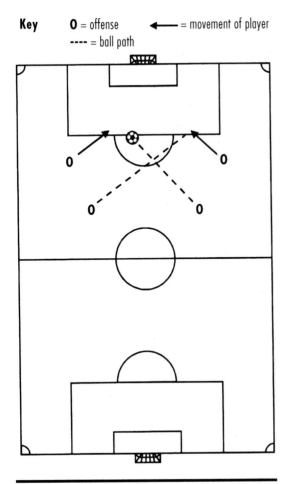

EXHIBIT 7.4   Looking for Open Space Drill

Looking for Open Space

Players on offense should be taught to look for open space. Indoor soccer is all about offense. When on offense, moving toward the goal, you must find open space. Players must learn to control the ball and pass to a teammate who is moving forward toward the goal with no defensive player covering him.

Looking for open space practices the skill of looking for a teammate who is at least 20 feet away and moving toward the goal. That player, in turn, gains control of the ball and passes on to the next player, 20 feet away. In both indoor and outdoor soccer, the player with the ball is looking to pass to an area where a teammate is heading, looking for a pass. It is like a football quarterback throwing to a spot he expects the receiver to reach when the ball gets there. In the same way, in soccer, the player with the ball doesn't pass the ball to another player, he passes it to a spot where another player is expected to be.

The objective is to practice long passes, while keeping control of the ball and scoring in mind. Looking for open space is also a great tool for teaching young players not to bunch up and have group chases toward a loose ball.

In this drill the players are about 20 feet apart, and the open space between them can result in a fast score if the kicker can get the ball quickly and accurately to a teammate.

Dancing with the Goalie

This is a corner-kick drill. Two offensive players line up near the goal, on either side of the goalie, and a third works the perimeter in front of the goal, ready to move toward the ball when it is kicked. The objective of player one is to block the goalie from defending against a ball entering the corner nearest to the kicker; the objective of player two is to keep the goalie from moving back to the center of the goal to defend a shot there. They constantly move their positions to keep the goalie guessing where he or she needs to go to defend the different areas. A third offensive player runs the perimeter of the goalie circle, waiting for a chance to score, while the teammates dance (gain position) with the goalie. The player doing the corner kick looks for the best opening, depending on which way the goalie is moving. She signals to her teammates whether she is kicking high or low, so two can block the goalie and the third can score.

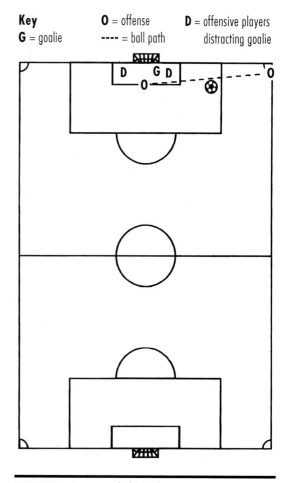

Key   **O** = offense   **D** = offensive players
G = goalie   **----** = ball path   distracting goalie

Player number 22 is dancing with the goalie, trying to block him from covering a kick that either number 40 or number 36 would receive from the corner kicker.

EXHIBIT 7.5   Dancing with the Goalie

As mentioned in Chapter 6, the coach should be alert to signs that players are getting tired of one drill and quickly change to another. You will soon recognize which are the drills your team considers the most fun. The best way to avoid boredom is to keep all of your players active, in motion, and in a competitive drill. Boredom sets in when you work with a few players while the others just stand around.

Evert Teunissen, professional indoor soccer coach and author of the book *Indoor Soccer*, urges coaches of youth soccer to be good observers of players in practice and in games and have a list of important instructions to call out when there is a situation in which they can help the player improve. The following is his list of the most helpful instructions he uses:

Take the ball where there's more room.

Look less at the ball and try to see where there is empty space.

Take the ball to an empty space quickly.

Use the leg and side of the foot closest to the ball.

Lower your center of gravity and use your arms for balance—you'll go faster.

If your foot's too tense you'll lose the ball.

Keep the ball next to your foot so you can turn or you'll lose it.

Slow down and view the field.

Slow down and dribble slowly.

Increase speed toward open spaces at the side.

Stop and turn; look for your teammates.

Stop and don't look at the ball.

Control the ball; change sides with the sole of your foot.

Pass the ball behind your support leg.

Bend your support leg and keep your body above the ball.

Game Strategies for Indoor Youth Soccer

The old adage "Your best defense is a good offense" has never been more true than when applied to indoor soccer. The Mexican name for it, *futbol rapido*, underscores the reason. The speed of the game quickly changes from offense to defense and back, literally within seconds. Even the goal-keeper becomes part of the offense when he or she kicks a well-aimed ball off the sideboard that ricochets to the mouth of the opposing goal. Not infrequently, it catches the other goalkeeper off guard, as the ball finds the goalkeeper's teammate in full stride toward the open space in front of the goal and goes in for a score. But in every instance, the defense becomes the offense when the goalie sends the ball toward the opposite goal into the scoring zone. To use a football expression, the "red zone" in indoor soccer is within 20 feet of the goal. To use a basketball analogy, a "fast break" occurs every time a defensive player controls a rebound of a shot on goal. With offside rarely called in indoor youth soccer, there is no way to stop the fast transition from defense to offense as there is in outdoor soccer where an offside call frequently foils a fast turnaround from defense to offense. You can't position a cherry picker, as is sometimes done in basketball. That would probably draw a call. It wouldn't be wise, in any case, since it would leave you shorthanded if you needed that player on defense. The strategy of trap, pass, and shoot works well in the World Cup, but for now let's stick to the real world of indoor youth soccer.

When your team goes on the offensive, you must tell the entire front line and the sweeper to push forward toward the goal. Ball control in the opponent's half of the playing field is the major objective. Watching the first few minutes of an indoor youth soccer game will normally establish which is the superior team, i.e., the team that controls the ball more in the oppo-nent's half of the field. "Time of possession," another football term the announcers use a lot, is analogous because in football as in soccer, the team that spends the most time in the opponent's half of the field usually ends up being the winning team.

CHAPTER 8

The best chance for a goal in indoor soccer is when you load the area in front of the net with your offensive players. The quicker your team sets up around the goal, the harder it is to defend against a shot on goal. So when your goalkeeper prepares to send the ball back down the floor, that's the signal for the offense to form. There is even a psychological advantage to a team being extra aggressive in pushing its offensive game. When your team is constantly pushing forward, the other team is forced back on its heels, backpedaling to defend its goal. Go to any indoor youth soccer game and you'll constantly hear the coach imploring the team to "push it up, push it up!"

In kids' soccer, missing the ball on an open net shot happens regularly. That's why it's important to have another player nearby to take a second shot; it's similar to the importance of rebounding in basketball. Tell your team to spread out as evenly as possible, and move quickly toward the goal kicking as soon as a shot is available. Coach them to anticipate rebound opportunities: off the back wall, off the goal, or off the goalie. Drill them in practice to handle all three opportunities to score. Rebounds are as important in indoor youth soccer as a good pass. Especially in U8 to U12, being in the right place at the right time is very important. Keep track of missed shots off rebounds and point those out to your team. Show them how many additional opportunities to score they missed. It's like keeping track of second shots off offensive rebounds in basketball.

Coach your players against bunching up. Just as in outdoor soccer, indoor position playing is important, perhaps even more so, as the playing area is so much smaller. Make sure that three offensive players are not all going for the ball in the corner, or chasing one defender, which leaves the other team wide open for passes and goals. Bunching up is a way of life in U6 and U8, because of the youth and inexperience of the players; but older players should know that bunching up, or group chasing, will cost them goals.

Passing the Ball Forward

When your team has control of the ball, your players should push the ball forward toward the defending goal, but without bunching up. They should try to keep extra defenders away from the ball. One on one is manageable, but if you let one of your players get isolated in a one-on-two situation, they risk losing the ball, unless the player in question is an exceptional ball handler. A good analogy would be in basketball, where a good ball-handling guard can keep his team in the game. In a indoor youth soccer game, a good dribbler and passer can keep his or her team in the game.

Strategy-wise, you as coach should determine in your practice sessions who your best ball handler is, and build your offense around him or her.

When that player moves toward the opposing goal, the rest of the team must join in pushing forward, including the defensive players.

More Shots Equal More Goals

It's as simple as that. Have an assistant coach keep the statistics of shots on goals by players to use in your next practice. Remind young players that they can't score unless they take shots. So convince the team to take as many shots on goal as possible. And they must be alert to react and converge on the goal every time a teammate takes a shot so as to be in position to control a rebound and a second shot. Again the analogy to basketball applies. How many times have you heard an NBA play-by-play announcer comment on the comparative statistics between the teams on capitalizing on offensive rebounds? Especially in the U8 and U12 age-groups, the more offensive players hovering around the goalmouth the better.

Off-the-Wall Strategy

In outdoor soccer, a good safe pass to the middle of the field is often the only pass possible. You will hear an outdoor soccer coach pleading to his players to get the ball in the middle. That is generally good strategy in indoor soccer, as well, but in indoor youth soccer, the coach should emphasize that the wall can add another player to your team, and slamming a ball off the wall to get it up the field may take advantage of the side lanes, whereas in outdoor soccer, the side lanes are often avoided, for fear of the ball going out of bounds.

This difference in strategy between indoor and outdoor soccer is not understood by many soccer moms (and dads), who are used to yelling "Kick it to the middle" when watching outdoor games, while their child's indoor soccer coach may be calling to use the side lanes.

Playing off the wall is an important drill for both the offense and the defense. The player who becomes adept at faking out an opposing player by kicking the ball off the wall to get around him, has learned a skill unique to the indoor game. As your players perfect this skill, you will notice how pleased they become with themselves. The defending player is never sure whether to play the ball, or move toward the wall to prevent the rebound, and once he or she commits to one or the other, the offensive player with the ball goes the opposite way and maintains control. Off-the-wall drills, both offensive and defensive, are important in practice sessions to perfect the rebound skill that is so useful in the indoor game.

A good pass off the corner wall that will ricochet the ball to a teammate in front of the goal, is a priceless move, almost impossible to defend against. As the players learn to play with each other, they should expect a pass off the wall and be ready for it. This is often where a good left-footed wing becomes a great impact player, receiving a rebound pass off the left wall.

In U8 and U12 indoor soccer, coaches shouldn't expect every pass to be perfect, whether it is a direct pass or a ricochet pass. However, because the playing field is so much smaller than that used in outdoor soccer, recovery from a bad pass is a lot quicker. Younger soccer players should be discouraged from making too many passes and attempts to set up. There always seems to be one pass too many, and then they lose the ball. Emphasize to players the importance of being aware of where they are in relation to the goal. And the three key things they should remember are:

1. Spread out; don't bunch up.
2. Take as many shots as possible.
3. Have a sense of where the goal is at all times.

Corner Kick Strategy

Corner kicks in indoor soccer offer great scoring opportunities. The strategy in this situation is to load up in front of the goal, as shown in Exhibit 8.1.

Have the player making the corner kick signal either high or low so teammates know where to be ready. Dancing with the goalie, which was explained in Chapter 7, is a good strategy on a corner kick. With two of your players essentially double-teaming the goalie, it immobilizes him so he can't react quickly to a shot on goal on either side of him. Coaches should be aware of who is their best kicker from the corner, because the corner kick comes into play many times during a indoor youth soccer game. Having a player who can kick the ball on the fly from the corner to the mouth of the goal gives your team a chance of scoring on every corner kick.

Heading off a high corner kick is popular, but a low kick in front of the goalmouth seems to work more consistently. Even if the ball is kicked around by the defense, there is still a good chance of a goal when the ball is in that area. There are nearly always good rebound opportunities in this situation. That is where you can justify overloading the red zone (the area within 20 feet of the mouth of the goal).

Key   **O** = offense   ---- = ball path

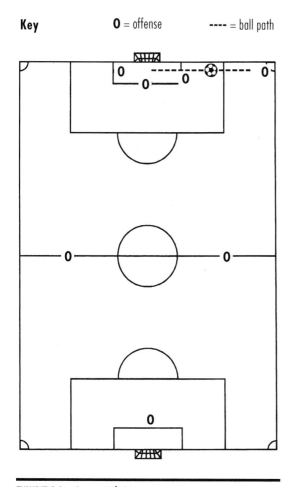

EXHIBIT 8.1   Corner Kick Strategy

Players 22 and 36 are in position to box-in the goalie when the ball is kicked from the corner, with player number 40 in position to score the goal.

Up-by-One Strategy

Your team is in a close game, and you are leading by one goal, with two minutes left on the clock. You are in the same situation as a professional football team that has to apply its play strategy to run out the clock. It calls for a conservative offense to maintain control of the ball, coupled with an aggressive defense to keep the ball out of your half of the playing field, where the other team could score.

Note the players' positions in Exhibit 8.2. You need your best goalie in the net, your sweeper on the midfield line, and your defensive players back from there about 10 to 15 feet to the right and left of the sweeper. Tell your sweeper and defensive players not to pass the midline. When the ball comes in their direction, they must concentrate on kicking it back into the opponents' side—no dribbling, no passing, no finessing. Your sweeper becomes a defense-only player in this important defensive strategy, which gives you three players on defense, whose only mission is to keep the ball from getting past them into their zone. The key is to regain control of the ball. The other team can't score from the opposite half of the arena, and they certainly can't score without possession of the ball.

Down-by-One Strategy

Now you are in the opposite situation, where the other team is up by one, and trying to run out the clock. There are two minutes left in the game, and your team is losing by a goal or two. You know you should win, but what can you do? Exhibit 8.3 has the answer.

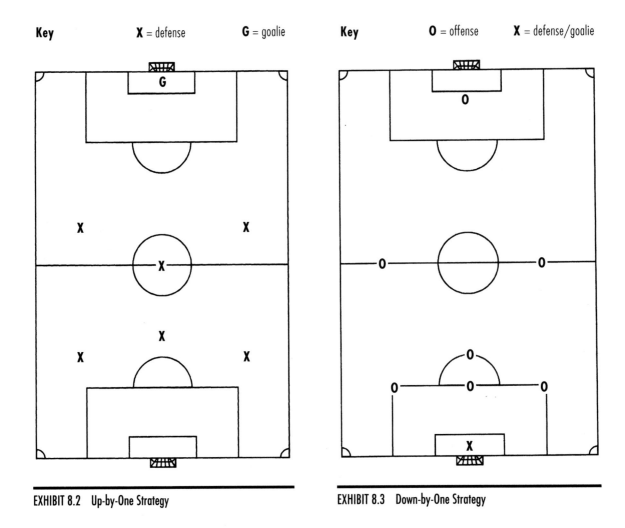

EXHIBIT 8.2 Up-by-One Strategy   **EXHIBIT 8.3 Down-by-One Strategy**

As soon as your team gets control of the ball, push your offense toward the defending goalie, and have your defense and sweeper line up at the midfield mark keeping the ball on your half of the floor. Your defenders must always keep the ball in front of them, as there is now nobody between them and your goalie. Your sweeper now moves forward with the rest of your offensive line. Keep the pressure on, and have your team take as many shots on goal as possible. Some coaches plan set plays. We have found that set plays, except for those to start a half, don't work in the pressure of a time constraint. In a down-by-one situation, with time running out, the best strategy is to keep the pressure on the opposition's goalie and take as many shots as possible.

You will note that your sweeper is the key strategist in both the up-by-one strategy, where she plays the role as the key defensive player, and in the down-by-one strategy, where she is the key offensive player. As coach, you must evaluate which of your players is up to these most important dual responsibilities. And having made that decision, you should spend extra time with your sweeper to make sure he or she understands the dual mission.

In-Your-Face Defensive Strategy

Now we are encouraging the same extra aggressiveness on defense, an in-your-face defense. It's like face-checking in a man-for-man defense in basketball.

You may think we are advocating that you try to have your team intimidate the opposition. We don't encourage rough play, but we do encourage coaching confidence in your players and getting them to recognize that if they dedicate themselves to practicing the drills and strategies you coach, they *will* have a winning season and be capable of beating any other team in their age class. Sometimes an opponent's team will have an outstanding player whose play must be neutralized. A good strategy would be to have your best player—usually your sweeper— assigned to apply an in-your-face defense against their best player's offense. In soccer this is called marking a player.

Good player defense in soccer is as important as defense in football. If the opposing team is allowed to play *their* game unstopped, there is little chance for your offense. But unlike football, in indoor soccer you don't have two teams, one for offense and the other for defense. If the other team

The defensive player is playing as close as possible to the player with the ball, without fouling him, to keep him from passing the ball and, hopefully, to steal the ball from him.

Here is an example where in-the-face guarding, on the part of the girl in the dark uniform, has resulted in stealing the ball from the boy in white.

has the ball, your entire team is on the defense. Coach your players to pick up an open man, and apply in-your-face pressure. Their offensive player cannot get a good shot on goal if your player is playing this type of defense.

Skull Sessions

From time to time we coaches use terms such as "sense of the floor," a "feel for the open space," and "a smell of the goal." They refer to the heady part of playing soccer—the intellectual understanding of the strategies of the game. Don't underestimate the smarts of your players; they may understand the strategies of the game more than you expect. The best way to find out, and to help you understand the level of smarts of your players, is to have skull sessions with them. Tell them you are appointing them all assistant coaches to help you. Then sit down with them with a diagram of the playing area, red and black checker markers to represent the players on both teams, and copies of the rulebook (and *this* book too!) at your side. Use the diagrams in this book to set up game situations, and create some others from actual games. Discuss with the team what their strategies should be. You may be pleasantly surprised at how much they know and who your best soccer brains turn out to be. Create some multiple-choice questions on a combination of the rules and strategies, and give out recognition stars to the players who achieve the best scores. The questions most often missed will give you an indication of the things you need to cover more in practice. Give your kids a chance to use their heads for more than just heading the ball and these skull sessions will pay off for your team.

CHAPTER 9

Indoor Youth Soccer Defense

When it comes to indoor soccer, we know that the best defense is a good offense. And we also know that every player goes on the offense when your team controls the ball, because of the small playing field. However, the opposite is just as true—and for the same reason. When the other team gets control and starts pushing the ball toward your goal, every player on your team must shift to defense. Basic indoor soccer strategy dictates that you should have two good kicking players back on defense at all times. However, a problem can arise when three or four offensive players confront your two defensive players before your team has regrouped and dropped back. This is why you should drill your entire team to drop back quickly and help on defense.

Often your players on offense will not drop back to help on defense, anticipating your team will regain possession and send them a long pass for an easy score. Point out to your team that this does not work, because (1) the opposing team will probably score first because your defense needed help, and (2) a long pass in that cherry-picking situation will usually be called an offside or a three-line pass.

It's the same problem in other sports; the offense gets the glory, so everyone wants to play offense. You need to teach your youth soccer team the importance of defense. In Chapter 12, "Winning," we suggest you give out stars to the players that have made outstanding plays during a game. The stars can be sewn onto the shoulders of their jerseys and can serve as great motivators. Be sure to give some stars for outstanding defensive plays as well as offensive scoring, and your defensive players will start to understand how important their role is. To the extent possible, give all of your players opportunities to play both offense and defense, but when you have settled on your best defensive players, make sure they understand how important they are to the team.

In indoor youth soccer, the 20-foot area in front of your goalie is the most dangerous. To use a football analogy, your defense should always keep the ball away from that red zone. "Clear the ball!" may be the most frequent call from the coach whose team is on defense in the red zone. Here is another difference in the strategy between outdoor and indoor youth soccer: in outdoor soccer, if your team is slow in the transition from offense to defense, you coach a player to deliberately kick the ball out of bounds to give your defense time to regroup. That's good strategy in outdoor soccer, but with no out-of-bounds in indoor soccer it's not valid. The closest thing to it would be an angle kick against the wall that will send the ball toward the other goal.

Given that most young players take their shots from the area in front of the goal, the defense should always keep the center clear. If they get control of the ball, they should not try anything fancy—just clear it to the corners, angle kick it, or try to push it out of their zone. Clearing it to the corner takes the immediate shot away from the other team and allows your team to reset and get the rest of your players in position to help clear the ball or gain control. If the offense is coming down the floor in any of the combinations of one-on-one, two-on-one, two-on-two, or three-on-one, the coach should stress to always try to take the ball away from the player with the ball and send it to the corner.

The defender, when he or she is confronted with an offensive player with the ball, should not consider that a one-on-one situation. It is essentially a challenge in which your team has a two-to-one advantage. However, that requires the defender and goalie to communicate and work together to prevent a goal. The goalie is in the same position as the catcher in baseball, with a runner on third trying to score. The goalie is facing the field and can see the entire play forming, so he or she must be the leader in directing teammates on what to do.

Your goalie will be able to spot your sweeper moving into position, which will soon give you three defenders, plus your goalie, in a diamond defense, the goalie and sweeper being the vertical points of the diamond, and the two defenders the horizontal points. The three defenders should be moving their points toward the center to block the lanes to the vulnerable front of the goal.

Keep the Goalie's Line of Vision Clear

Don't let your goalie get blindsided by an unexpected shot. Your goalie may be involved in an offensive move by the other team in which one player is blocking the goalie's line of vision while the other is shooting. Your players should counteract that move by keeping the open lanes blocked and allowing your goalie to move into a position where his or her vision is not blocked. Earlier in the book we spoke about your sweeper being fast and able to move easily in any direction. There is no more important defensive role for the sweeper than clearing the ball out of the area in front of the goal. Let your players know how important their role is in helping their goalie and preventing the other team from scoring.

Cover the Open Space

When the ball is in the critical 20-foot area in front of the goal, both teams will be playing to the open space. That means your players must not only cover each offensive player in that zone, one to one, but also must cover the open space where they want to go. That's when the sweeper has to be ready to switch quickly from offensive mode to defensive mode. In this respect, he or she is the playmaker not only on offense, but also on defense. The sweeper must carry the ball forward and start an offensive play.

Opening Game Defense

The referee starts the game with a coin toss. When the other team wins and goes on offense first, how should you position your team to defend? Remember that your whole team goes into defense mode when the opposing team has control of the ball.

In this situation, your center and two forwards should drop back about 10 feet. That puts them in the position to intercept a hard kick toward your goal. If the opposing team starts with a short pass, instruct your team not to try to steal. They should wait for the other team to bring the ball into your end. Chasing down the first pass will only catch you shorthanded early in the game.

Try to get your sweeper to move quickly after the ball when it comes into your end, and to keep control of the ball until your team reverses field and moves into the other team's end. Remember the best defense in the early stages of the game is getting control of the ball and moving it into the other half of the playing field, as your offense moves into attack mode.

The percentages in all sports show that the team that scores first usually wins, so psychologically you don't want the opposition to get a shot on goal on their first touch of the ball. Let your team know how important it is to score first and,

Key
O = team A
X = team B
G = goalies

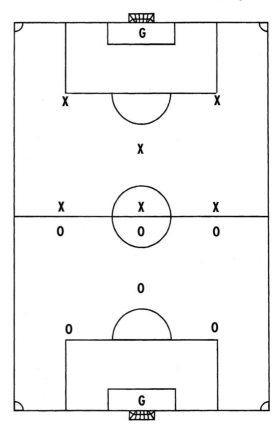

EXHIBIT 9.1   Starting the Game on Defense

conversely, how focused they must be on defense to prevent a first goal by the opposition.

Penalty Kick Defense

Penalty kicks in general are like the foul shot in basketball or the extra point in football. It should be an automatic score. In indoor youth competition the penalty kick generally is an easy goal, with not much the goalie can do but hope he or she guesses correctly where the ball will be aimed. The opposing team generally uses their best offensive player from the distance set by your league (usually 10 or 12 yards out). The experienced goalie tries to move back and forth in front of the goal, trying to confuse the kicker, while at the same time trying to guess, by reading the eyes of the kicker, where the ball will be kicked: left or right, up or down. But even a correct guess doesn't guarantee a save on a kick from that short distance. The goalie who successfully defends against a penalty kick deserves to be considered for the MVP award for the game.

Key
O = offense
X = defense
G = goalie
- - - - = ball path

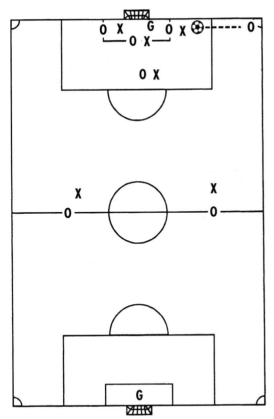

EXHIBIT 9.2   Defense Against Corner Kick

Corner Kick Defense

A corner kick is almost as dangerous as a penalty kick. The offense takes a kick from the corner and usually has a set play to run, which includes loading up the area in front of the goal. The best defense for that situation is to play one-to-one coverage, with players using their body as a barrier between the ball and the goal when the player they are guarding has the ball. Assign your players to similar opposing players—i.e., same speed, same height, and so on. In soccer, you are always looking for either a defensive or offensive advantage.

Your team is at a defensive disadvantage, so your best strategy is to neutralize their offensive advantage by playing a one-to-one in-your-face defense. As in many other defensive situations, your objective should be to clear the area in front of the goal and keep your goalie's line of sight open. As soon as one of your players touches the ball, he or she should try to clear it out of your zone by kicking it toward the opposite end or slamming it against the wall at an angle that will send it into open space near one of your other players.

Goalie Skills

Like a pitcher in baseball, the goalie in soccer wants a shutout—or as close to a shutout as possible. In both cases, the pitcher and the goalie are depending on their hitters to score, and secure the win. In another analogy, the soccer goalie is like the baseball catcher. Like the catcher, the goalie can see the whole field and both teams. Also, like the catcher, he or she must be the take-charge player, barking directions to teammates to help protect the goal.

Diving

The goalie is also like the shortstop in baseball—ready to dive either left or right to make a saving catch. The goalie must react quickly as a ball comes speeding at the goal, and in a continuous motion get the ball going in the opposite direction toward an open space by either throwing it out to a team-mate or punting it down field. You should coach your goalie never to punt down field in the middle. Always punt to one side or the other. This is one difference between outdoor and indoor soccer. Goalies in outdoor soccer avoid kicking to the side lanes because of the risk of the ball going out of bounds.

Catching the Ball

This is the ideal defense for the goalie. He or she regains control of the ball and stops the offensive momentum of the opponents. When a shot is taken on goal, the goalie's first line of defense is to catch the ball, making a W with his or her two hands, thumbs together, palms up, and fingers spread as wide as possible. After catching the ball, the goalie should pull it tightly to his body to prevent it from slipping out and returning to play. Reaction time is important because not only must the goalie stop the offensive thrust, but he or she must also take advantage of the change in control of the ball, and get the ball moving quickly in the other direction before the other team has the time to regroup into defensive mode. In evaluating potential goalies, the coach should look for players with big hands, long fingers, and aggressive leadership skills. Also look for players who don't mind diving, falling, or getting in the way of a fast-moving ball. The goalie in soccer is like the catcher in baseball; in both cases they have to able to take a beating. Anyone who has coached both baseball and soccer will understand the type of player needed for the goalie position. Some players on your team may be attracted by the fancy shirt and gloves, but not every youngster can take the rough-and-tumble life of a goalie. There is a lot of pressure on the goalie because he or she is often in the hot seat with respect to the outcome of the game. It is not at all uncommon for a sensitive youngster to dissolve into

The goalie makes a W with his two gloved hands to make sure both hands are in position to get a firm grip on the ball or to deflect it if the ball cannot be caught.

The goalie has caught the ball securely with both hands and must now look up the field for the best way to put the ball in play in the opposite direction.

tears, feeling he has let down his teammates when the team loses a close game. The caring coach has to restore the goalie's confidence, while at the same time making sure none of the other players on the team get on the goalie's case. The goalie should keep his entire body in front of the ball to act as a second barrier to prevent the ball from going through the goal. When the ball is kicked directly at the goalie, and can be caught, she should have her arms in position to bring the ball into her body, braced to receive it. On high balls, the goalie should meet the ball at the apex of its flight, deciding as he jumps whether to deflect it over the goal (if he's concerned that he might not be able to catch it). If the ball is low, the goalie should come out to meet it, rather than waiting for it to come to her, and be ready to scoop it up and in one motion throw or kick it in the other direction. If it is coming hard, fast, and low, the goalie should get his body low and try to catch it, absorbing the speed of the ball with his body. At any height or speed, the ball should be caught rather than just deflected, if at all possible. The goalie must control the ball after catching it, which is always a goalie's best defense. Then she must instantaneously change the mode from defense to offense and move the ball to her teammates so they can maintain possession.

Punching or Tipping

Coach your goalie to punch the ball into a safe area, when it is obvious it can't be caught; this is a great strategy for making a save. It is a good defense against a corner kick where the ball is kicked in the air in front of a crowded goal. Teach the goalie to punch the ball by placing the fists together and punching as if the two hands are glued together. Caution him or her to tuck the thumbs back to protect them against injury during punching. Sometimes a goalie will use only one fist when he or she can't reach the ball with both fists. A coach should constantly remind the goalie, "When in doubt, punch!" The goalie should be taught to punch the ball to the side, high and far, so that it can't be controlled by an offensive player for another quick shot at the goal.

When the ball is out of the range for a sure catch, this tipping is a technique that can alter the path of the ball. Tipping the ball outside of the vertical or horizontal goal post is done with the fingertips, not the whole hand. It is important that the goalie understands that tipping is designed just to alter the ball's path, not its speed. Altering the speed may just drop the ball and allow it to pass under the horizontal goal post, which is more likely to occur if the goalie uses his or her whole hand.

The goalie's last resort should always be punching the ball over the net on a high shot, or tipping a shot off to the side on a shot in either corner. However, she must always be ready for a rebound shot in this situation. Unlike in outdoor soccer, where a high or wide shot usually goes out of bounds, with indoor soccer the ball will hit off the boards and give the opposition an immediate rebound shot. Judging the height and angle of a bounced ball toward the goal area is critical. Jumping to catch the ball too soon, too late, too low, or too high can result in an embarrassing goal. It is a goalie skill that only repetitive drills of shots on goal will perfect.

Catching Low Balls

The goalie should be coached to get directly behind the ball and bring the legs together, while bending over. After catching the ball, he or she should bring it into the midsection or chest. Coach against becoming complacent about what may appear to be an easy save. Total concentration on the ball, wherever it is coming, high or low, slow or fast, is of paramount importance for the goalie.

Punting

Young, inexperienced goalies tend to punt the ball nearly every time they get possession of it. They should be taught the other options and when each makes the most sense. Most important is the skill of scanning the field and making the quick decision of where is the best place to send the ball (and then how best to get it there). There is no question that a long, hard punt that will carry the ball some distance down the field is a good play, but only if the goalie has practiced it many times and can execute it consistently. The punting foot should contact the ball at the bony part of the instep after being dropped only a few inches. Eyes should be kept on the ball. A nearly forgotten but very useful kicking skill is drop kicking. Teach your goalies how to drop kick to give them another weapon in their arsenal of defense.

Goal Kicking

If another player is a better kicker than the goalie, it is a temptation for the coach to have that player make the goal kick, with the goalie just standing by. That is poor strategy for two reasons: (1) it wastes valuable time waiting for the other player to return to the goal area to make the kick, time during which the other team can move into a defensive position, and (2) it shorts your team one player on offense by preventing the kicker from moving down field as a part of the offense.

The coaching solution is to make your goalie practice kicking more until he or she becomes your best kicker, or is at least good enough that on balance it is better for the goalie to kick the ball and allow your other player to assume his or her regular position.

Cutting Down the Angle

The goalie must cut the corners down on the offensive players trying to score. Use a geometry exercise on your clipboard to illustrate how the open space available in the goal for scoring changes as the goalie cuts the potential angle of the kick. This analogy works better as the players get older and understand the basics of angles and geometry. The goalie must cut down the size of the open space by giving the opponent a less desirable shot angle. After catching the ball, the goalie must decide whether to punt, pass, or drop kick the ball. The goalie should look to the sides, rather than the center for the outlet, as kicking the ball in the center may result in another offensive run at the goal. In indoor soccer the walls offer the unique opportunity for angle kicks, again demonstrating a unique advantage the indoor goalie has over his outdoor-soccer counterpart.

The Tough Side of Being a Goalie

Being a goalie is a tough job, and it's especially tough in indoor soccer. The goalie must dive to make saves on a hard floor, not soft grass. Opposing players are much closer when they shoot, and the indoor goalie must get rid of the ball quicker, which can lead to mistakes. The mission is to protect the goal, cut down the angles, make the catch, make the save, take charge, keep possession, and get the ball quickly to teammates as they move into the offensive mode.

Because the indoor game moves so quickly, the goalie must always be alert and have a high level of concentration. That's a tall order for players in the U10-and-below age range. Fulfilling it demands practice, practice, practice.

As a coach, you should let all your players try out for the goalie position. Quickness and jumping ability are several traits you should measure. Some kids are just attracted by the fancy shirt and gloves the goalie wears, but the novelty wears off when the rougher aspects of goaltending reveal themselves. In baseball, the prototype of a catcher is a big, strong player. In soccer, there should be no such prototype. A big player does have an advantage on defending against high kicks but may give up quickness and mobility in comparison to a smaller player. In any event, a coach should pick more than one goalie so as to have backups in case one misses a game or is hurt. Frequently your best goalie may also be your best overall player— for example, your sweeper or your center. You can't waste this player's offensive skills by making him or her play goalie the whole game. However, you may have a situation, often late in a close game, where your best player is tiring. At that point it would be good strategy to put that player in the goal to rest, and also take advantage of his or her good defensive skills.

Coaches should remember to praise the goalie even after a loss. A loss usually is not the goalie's fault; more often it can be traced to a lack of defense or inability to clear the ball. However, the player who was in the goal when the winning score went in usually feels bad, and often this player thinks he or she cost the team the game. With younger players the tears sometimes start flowing in this situation. This is where the coach must step in and make the player feel better. Explain that the outcome of the game was not the goalie's fault, that soccer is a team sport, and that the team was not always in the right place at the right time. If you don't help to make the goalie feel better, he or she might never put on the gloves again. You may also face some negative reactions from the parents, particularly if the player was reduced to tears. But most often you can diffuse that by showing them your caring side.

CHAPTER 10

The Official Rules of Indoor Soccer

In the popular McGraw-Hill book on outdoor youth soccer, *The Baffled Parent's Guide to Coaching Youth Soccer*, author Bobby Clark says, "Rules for youngsters should be kept to a minimum. I am a great believer in small-sided games in which there is no offside rule." We wholeheartedly agree, and indoor youth soccer fulfills the "small-sided games" part, as there are only five to seven players on an indoor soccer team. He goes on to say, "Each league will have its own rules, as well." Again we agree, and we urge new coaches to become familiar with their local rules. In many cases they will include a *no-offside rule*, or officials will rarely call it in U12 and younger games.

In deference to first-time baffled parent/coaches who may be unfamiliar with both outdoor and indoor soccer, we think it is only fair to provide a framework of the basic rules for indoor soccer. To someone who is familiar with outdoor soccer rules, it would be wise to study these indoor soccer rules, as there are some significant differences. We also believe it's prudent for a coach to explain the basic rules to new players, both those who have played outdoor soccer, and to those who may not. Sometimes youngsters in their youthful exuberance commit fouls without realizing they are fouls.

It has been only in recent years that soccer rules were published. Previously, soccer organizations referred to them as "The Laws of Soccer" (and some still do). It is just one indication of how seriously professional adults have always regarded the game of soccer.

But whether they are called laws or rules, they spell out the framework of how the game should be played, and the penalties imposed when the rules are not observed. The United States Indoor Soccer Association is the organization that has framed and published "The Official Rules of Indoor Soccer." We know of no other source. There are two editions, Professional, and Youth and Amateur. The abridged version of the latter is the one we will be reviewing, as it applies to the subject of this book: youth indoor soccer. *The Unabridged Official Rules of Indoor Soccer, Youth and Amateur Edition,* is an easy-to-read, pocket-size booklet of 22 pages. No good coach should show up at the soccer arena without it.

    With the permission of the United States Indoor Soccer Association, we are quoting, from the abridged edition, the most significant of the rules. (To order a copy of the unabridged edition, containing the full set of rules, contact the USISA at www.usindoor.com.)

Rule 1: The Field of Play

Owing to structural differences among indoor soccer facilities, the following provisions constitute generally accepted standards for field dimensions, walls, goals, and markings.

Field Dimensions: The field of play shall be adapted for the size of the facility, with dimensions between 140 and 210 feet in length and 60 and 90 feet in width. The standard dimensions are 180 feet by 75 feet, with corners rounded in the arc of a circle having a 28-foot radius. Exhibit 10.1 shows the official field diagram. (All of the action diagrams in the book show a scaled-down version of the field of play.)

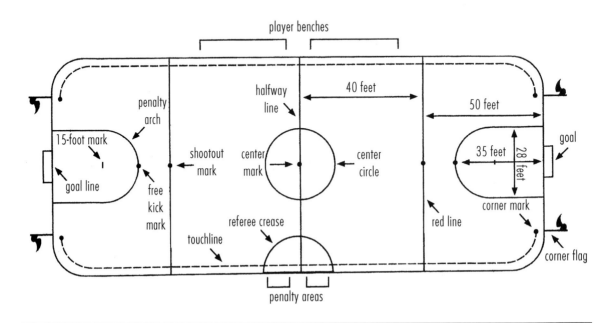

EXHIBIT 10.1   The Field of Play

Perimeter Wall: The field of play is enclosed by a perimeter wall, which is part of the playing surface. The wall is 4 to 12 feet high, with the standard being 8 feet, except above the goals (2 feet above the crossbar) and along the team benches (4 feet).

Goals: The standard goal dimensions are 12 feet wide by 6½ feet high. The foremost outside contours for the goalposts and crossbar are smooth and flush with the plane of the perimeter wall. (Note this is approximately one-half the width of an outdoor soccer goal and not as high.)

Rule 2: The Ball

The ball is size 4 indoor for U12 and below and size 5 for all others.

Rule 3: The Players

Teams U12 and below have no fewer than 5 or more than 7 players on the field at a time, including a goalkeeper. For above U12, no fewer than 4 or more than 6 are allowed. During an overtime period, neither team shall play with more than the minimum provided.

Each team may substitute players freely, provided that (a) players must substitute off the field of play or within the touch line in the area of their team bench, and (b) no substitutions are allowed during an overtime period or during the first 3 seconds of a shootout.

Rule 4: The Players' Equipment

Players wear their team's uniform, consisting of the same colors, shin guards, and indoor footwear. The goalkeeper wears jersey colors distinguished from all other field players and from the referees.

Rule 5: The Referee

One (1) referee officiates each game. A second floor referee, an assistant referee, and a timekeeper, may assist the referee.

Rule 6: The Duration of the Game

A regulation game consists of 24-minute halves, subject to "house rules" and the following:

(a) Overtime period and tiebreaker: If, in a tournament or playoff, the game is tied at the end of regulation, a 10-minute "sudden death" overtime period follows. If still tied at the end of the overtime period, a tiebreaker ensues under Rule 12.

(b) Running clock: Except in the case of an unusual delay, determined by the referee, the game clock counts down continuously through each half or overtime period.

Rule 7: The Start and Restart of Play

A kickoff from the center mark starts play at the beginning of each half and after every goal. A dropped ball starts play at the beginning of any overtime period. A player who starts play may not again play the ball until it touches another player.

The referee designates the team to take the first half kickoff and the end of the field each team shall defend (according to house rules). For the start of the second half, the teams change defensive ends, and the kickoff is taken by the team other than that which took it in the first half.

The referee signals a restart.

Restarts take place by either a kickoff, free kick, goalkeeper throw-in, or dropped ball. Other than for kickoffs or as provided below, restarts occur within 3 feet from the spot of the ball at the moment of stoppage.

A team receives a free kick after stoppages other than when a dropped ball or goalkeeper throw-in is required. Before the team takes the free kick, the ball must be stationary. All opposing players are at least 15 feet from the spot of the free kick (or, if within 15 feet of the opponent's goal, along the goal line) until after the restart. The spot of the free kick is that provided above, except:

(a) Within own penalty arch: from any spot therein;

(b) Within opponent's penalty arch: from the free kick mark ("top of the arch");

(c) Illegal pass back to goalkeeper: from the goalkeeper's free kick mark;

(d) Delayed penalty:
  (i) according to the ensuing stoppage, as normally administered, or
  (ii) in case the defending team obtains possession of the ball during play, from the spot of the original offense. If the original offense would have resulted in a shootout, but for the delayed penalty, the restart is a shootout, except when the attacking team scores or commits a foul or carded offense, in which case (i) applies.

(e) Penalty kick or shootout: see Rule 12;

(f) Kick-in: from the point on the touch line nearest where the ball crossed over the wall;

(g) Corner kick: from the corner mark nearest to where the ball exited play;

(h) Goalkeeper throw-in: see below;

(i) Three-line violation: from the offending team's restart mark;

(j) Superstructure violation: from the nearer restart mark.

If neither team has clear possession of the ball at a stoppage, the referee restarts play with a dropped ball. A dropped ball caused while the ball is inside a penalty arch takes place at the nearer free kick mark.

Play restarts with a goalkeeper throw-in anywhere within the penalty arch after an attacking player has last touched the ball before crossing an end perimeter wall.

Rule 8: The Ball in and out of Play

A three-line violation occurs when a player propels the ball in the air across the two red lines and the halfway line toward the opponent's goal without touching the perimeter wall, another player, or a referee on the field of play.

A superstructure violation occurs when the ball contacts any part of the building above the field of play.

Rule 9: The Method of Scoring

A team scores a goal when the whole of the ball legally passes over the goal line. A goal may be scored directly from a kickoff or restart.

Rule 10: Fouls and Other Violations

Fouls: A foul occurs if a player:

(a) Holds an opponent;
(b) Handles the ball (except by the goalkeeper within his penalty arch);
(c) Plays in a dangerous manner;
(d) Slide tackles;
(e) Impedes the progress of an opponent ("obstruction"); or
(f) Prevents the goalkeeper from releasing the ball from his hands;

and when a player commits the following in a manner that the referee considers careless, serious, reckless, or involving excessive force:

(a) Kicks an opponent;
(b) Trips an opponent;
(c) Jumps at an opponent;
(d) Charges an opponent;
(e) Strikes or elbows an opponent; or
(f) Pushes an opponent.

Unsporting Behavior: A free kick results for the following offenses:

(a) Leverage: using the body of a teammate to propel oneself to head the ball;
(b) Encroachment: entering the protected area of an opposing player taking a free kick (after initial warning);

(c) Trickery: passing the ball back to a goalkeeper by "trickery";

(d) Dissent:

    (i) referee abuse;

    (ii) breach of penalty area decorum; or

    (iii) entering the Referee crease without permission;

(e) Other: Behavior which, in the referee's discretion, does not warrant another category of penalty (e.g., taunting, foul language).

Goalkeeper Violations: The opposing team receives a free kick for the following violations by a goalkeeper:

(a) Illegal handling: bringing the ball from outside of the penalty arch to his hand within it, or receiving the ball again after a goalkeeper throw-in, without the ball's having first touched another player;

(b) Pass back: handling the ball, having been passed deliberately and directly to him by a teammate, except that he may handle a ball that a teammate passes to him by the head, chest, or knee and without "trickery" (the use of a wall or foot to flick the ball to a head, chest, or knee before making the pass);

(c) 5-seconds: controlling the ball with either his hand or foot inside of his penalty arch for more than 5 seconds.

Team Violations: The referee issues a team penalty for the following violations by a team or unidentified person:

(a) Leaving team bench: players leave a team bench to join a fracas, melee, or confrontation with the opposition or a game official;

(b) Bench dissent: after an initial "warning" issued to the team captain, one or more players from a team bench verbally abuse the referee; or

(c) Other: unsporting behavior, which, in the referee's discretion, does not warrant another category of penalty.

Advantage Rule: The referee allows play to continue, notwithstanding the commission of an offense, when the team against which it has been committed will benefit from an existing offensive advantage. In the case of carded offenses, see Rule 11.

Flagrant Fouls: A penalty kick is awarded for the following fouls committed by a defender in his defensive half of the field:

(a) A foul within the penalty arch or goal for which he receives a time penalty;

(b) A foul from behind, against an attacking player, having control of the ball and one or no defensive players between himself and the goal; or

(c) Any foul where he is the last player on his team between the attacking player with the ball and the goal.

Blue Card Offenses: Unless otherwise provided below, the referee issues a blue card for serious fouls and for:

(a) Deliberate handball or handball by a goalkeeper;

(b) Goalkeeper endangerment;

(c) Boarding;

(d) Unsporting behavior by a player; or

(e) Team violations.

Cautionable Offenses: The referee issues a yellow card for reckless fouls and offenses described directly above, and for the following:

(a) Second blue card;

(b) Unsporting behavior by any team personnel; or

(c) Provoking altercation: making physical contact with an opponent (e.g., pushing or poking), short of fighting, or using the ball in so doing.

Ejectionable Offenses: A person receives a red card for fouls and offenses described directly above that the referee considers violent or use of excessive force, and for:

(a) Second yellow card;

(b) Third time penalty;

(c) Elbowing: intentionally elbowing an opponent above the shoulder;

(d) Vicious slide tackling: a tackle from the side or from behind directly into one or both legs of an opponent, seriously endangering him;

(e) Fighting;

(f) Leaving team bench of penalty area to engage in a fracas, melee, or confrontation with the opposition or a game official; or

(g) Extreme unsporting behavior: committing particularly despicable behavior, including:

(i)   spitting at an opponent or any other person;

(ii) persistent use of extremely abusive language or behavior toward a game official; or

(iii) bodily contact with a game official in dissent.

Rule 11: Time Penalties

It should be noted that time penalties are often waived in youth competition at the U12 level and below in local play, but may be enforced in tournaments. A coach is well advised to inquire about the application of time penalties at the start of the season, and at the start of a tournament.

The following penalties apply to offenses for which a card is issued (subject to further action by the administrative authority):

(a) Blue card: 2 minutes (i.e., in the penalty area);

(b) Yellow card: 2 minutes;

(c) Red card (for accumulation of cards by player): 2 minutes, plus ejection;

(d) Other red card: 5 minutes, plus ejection.

The person who commits a carded offense serves the penalty, except for players designated by their teams to serve time penalties of their team, their goalkeeper, nonplayer personnel, and teammates who receive red cards. Otherwise, players serve their time penalties until their expiration and the referee permits their release.

Short-Handed Play: For each time penalty being served by a player, his team shall play with one fewer field player until its expiration; provided that a team may not have fewer than the minimum required, regardless of the number serving time penalties. Should a player receive a time penalty, while two or more teammates are already in the penalty area, his team continues to play with the minimum while he joins his teammates in the area.

Under the following circumstances, time penalties either expire prior to their completed countdown, or have the beginning of their countdowns delayed:

(a) Powerplay goal: If a team is scored upon having fewer players on the field of play, due to one or more players serving time penalties, a player from the team is released from the penalty area into the field of play, unless otherwise prohibited, and the player's penalty or penalties are wiped out. If the team has two players in the penalty area, only the player whose time penalty or penalties are recorded earlier is affected.

(b) Delayed penalty: See below.

(c) Multiple penalties: If two teammates are serving time penalties when another teammate is penalized, his time penalty does not begin to count down until at least one of the teammates' time penalties has expired and his time penalty is next to begin.

(d) Release of teammates serving simultaneous time penalties: When two or more teammates' time penalties expire simultaneously, the order in which they are recorded dictates the order of their release.

(e) Simultaneous ejections: When two simultaneous red cards carrying the same time penalties are assessed to opposing players, their time penalties are not served.

(f) Maximum time penalty: No player may receive more than 5 minutes for penalties arising at the same time on the game clock, irrespective of the number or nature of accumulated offenses or the fact that one or more teammates may be designated to serve such time.

(g) End of game: All time penalties carry over between periods and expire at the end of the game.

Delayed Penalty: In instances where the referee would issue a blue card or a yellow card, but for the advantage rule, he acknowledges the offense by holding the card above his head until the earlier to occur of the following:

(a) Opponent's possession: the team of the offending player gains control of the ball; or

(b) Stoppage: the referee stops play for any reason.

Once play is stopped, the offense is recorded and assessed, as customary. In the event of a powerplay goal, the provisions regarding early expiration of time penalties remain applicable.

Rule 12: Penalty Kicks and Shootouts

Penalty Kick: All players of the attacking team stand behind the halfway line and outside of the center circle. Players of the defending team stand behind the halfway line and inside of the center circle.

(a) The ball is placed at the free kick mark nearer the attacking goal (top of the arch).

(b) The goalkeeper has at least one foot on his goal line and may not move off it until after the referee whistles the penalty kick to begin and the ball is in play.

The referee whistles that the play is dead before signaling that a tripping foul has been committed.

(c) Once the referee whistles the penalty kick to begin, the player taking the penalty kick (whom the kicking team is free to designate) has 5 seconds to strike the ball, restarting play.

(d) The player taking the penalty kick may not touch the ball again until it has been touched by another player.

Shootout:

(a) All players serving time penalties sit in their appropriate penalty area. All players of the attacking team stand behind the halfway line and outside of the center circle. Players of the defending team stand behind the halfway line and inside of the center circle.

(b) The ball is placed at the restart mark nearer the attacking goal.

(c) The goalkeeper has at least one foot on his goal line and may not move off of it until after the referee whistles the shootout to begin.

(d) Once the referee whistles the shootout to begin, the ball is "in play" and the player taking the shootout plays the ball forward using any legal manner to score (e.g., direct shot on goal, dribbling and shooting, playing the ball off the boards, passing to a teammate, etc.).

Tiebreaker: A tiebreaker proceeds by shootouts, except that:

(a) The referee designates the goal at which both teams shoot and the team that shoots first (according to administrative policy).

(b) All players, other than the player taking the shot and the defending goalkeeper, remain within their team bench areas.

(c) Both teams have up to 3 shots, with players from each team kicking alternately.

(d) If, at any time, a team obtains a 2-goal advantage, the tiebreaker ceases and the winner is declared.

(e) If, after both teams have taken 3 shots, neither has an advantage, the tiebreaker continues, alternating one player at a time, until both teams have taken an equal number of shots and one team has scored when the other has not.

(f) The player has 5 seconds to score after the referee's whistle.

If these rules tend to confuse you, relax. The more you are around indoor soccer, the more the written rules will make sense to you. Recognize that at least you will know more about them than your players do, and probably more than your players' parents do. Get yourself a copy of the complete Official Rules of Indoor Soccer from the United States Indoor Soccer Association and study them. If you have questions, buy a referee a cup of coffee and pick his brain a bit. If that doesn't help, contact the United States Indoor Soccer Association at www.usindoor.com.

Exhibit 10.2 shows the referee signals with which soccer coaches must become familiar.

EXHIBIT 10.2   Referee Signals

CHAPTER 11

Dealing with Parents and Pressure

The two *Ps*, *Parents* and *Pressure*, belong together in a book on youth sports, because, to some extent, they represent a cause-and-effect problem for parents and their children. In addition to parents' pressure, coaches' pressure can also add to an unhealthy situation for sensitive children. Unfortunately that situation, in one form or another, has plagued many well-meaning youth sports organizations. It reached tragic proportions in the well-publicized incident in Massachusetts, in which a youth hockey coach was murdered by another father in a fit of rage during a confrontation over their sons' youth hockey game. More recently there was the report of a free-for-all among parents, coaches, and players at a youth football game in California.

It has been called Little League rage in baseball, but some soccer moms and dads have been getting carried away during youth soccer games. In the September 15, 2002, issue of the *Washington Post*, there was an article describing the steps that the suburban Montgomery County, Maryland, Soccer League (Montgomery Soccer Inc.) has been required to adopt to curb a disturbing trend of misbehavior among coaches and parents, including fighting, taunting, and racial insults. The organization's newsletter chastised the guilty parties: "We'd really prefer it if our coaches and parents could come to the realization, without our help, that they should act like adults." The help the league is providing to remind them they are adults and the players are children (their children) is the organization of volunteer team-sportsmanship liaisons, formed by more levelheaded concerned parents. They monitor games and file reports to the league, rating the sportsmanship of each team and its fans. The article went on to say that the idea of team-sportsmanship liaisons works well for the National Capital Soccer League, which began monitoring parents' behavior in 1998.

Sports Illustrated published a special edition in 1999 titled, "Do you know who is coaching your child?" It featured true stories of convicted child molesters who were coaching youth sports teams and underscored the terrifying fact that many youth sports organizations, in their frantic efforts to recruit volunteers, make no effort either to screen or monitor them to make sure they will be positive role models for children. While parents are comforted by the fact their children's teachers must be fingerprinted and screened by police, they have ignored the fact that volunteer coaches, who spend nearly as much time with their children as teachers, are neither screened nor even very closely supervised. This is why the coaches from NYSCA (National Youth Soccer Coaches Association), an affiliate of the National Alliance of Youth Sports (NAYS), are routinely subjected to finger-printing and background checks. NYSCA advises its leagues that as little as a one-dollar addition to the registration fee will be sufficient to fund finger-printing and background checking procedures. Little League, Inc., has followed NAYS in requiring background checks and fingerprinting of all managers and coaches, announcing that this requirement will be added to the Little League Baseball 2003 Rules Book.

Also in 1999, a landmark book was published entitled *Why Johnny Hates Sports*. It was authored by Fred Engh, formerly of Ocean City, Maryland, and now president of NAYS. The book's subtitle was *Why Organized Youth Sports Are Failing Our Children and What We Can Do About It*. The simple answer to his question of why so many youngsters get turned off to youth sports is because many adults—parents and coaches—take the fun out of kids sports. His book is not only an expose of the ugly side of youth sports, but it also provides a solution to solving the complex problems of parents and/or coaches who make youth sports unattractive to the very children they ostensibly want to help.

It is no coincidence that we chose Ocean City, Maryland, Engh's former home, as the backdrop for this book. As mentioned earlier, the managers of the Ocean City Recreation Complex have embraced the positive philosophy of NAYS in their youth sports program.

Engh quoted a comprehensive study of youth sports, which was conducted by the Youth Sports Institute at Michigan State University. It listed the top 10 reasons why boys and girls dropped out of youth sports. The top three responses given by both genders were: "It was no longer fun," "There was too much pressure [parental and coach]," and "The coach was a poor role model." The remedial program NAYS initiated includes parent education and commitment to positive and objective goals for children. Included is a Parent's Code of Ethics (Exhibit 11.1), which parents are asked to sign after a meeting at which their children's team manager explains the goals and philosophy of the league.

Some leagues make attendance at a parent meeting mandatory if the parents want their child to participate. One of the most significant points in the Parent's Code of Ethics is: "I will place the emotional and physical well-being of my child ahead of a personal desire to win."

Parent's Code of Ethics

I hereby pledge to provide positive support, care, and encouragement for my child participating in youth sports by following this Parent's Code of Ethics:

- I will encourage good sportsmanship by demonstrating positive support for all players, coaches, and officials at every game, practice, or other youth sports event.

- I will place the emotional and physical well-being of my child ahead of my personal desire to win.

- I will insist that my child play in a safe and healthy environment.

- I will require that my child's coach be trained in the responsibilities of being a youth sports coach and that the coach upholds the Coaches' Code of Ethics.

- I will demand a sports environment for my child that is free from drugs, tobacco, and alcohol, and will refrain from their use at all youth sports events.

- I will remember that the game is for youth—not adults.

- I will do my very best to make youth sports fun for my child.

- I will ask my child to treat other players, coaches, fans, and officials with respect, regardless of race, sex, creed, or ability.

- I will read the NYSCA National Standards for Youth Sports, and do what I can to help all youth sports organizations implement and enforce them.

_____   _____
Signature   Date

EXHIBIT 11.1   Parent's Code of Ethics

A companion Coaches' Code of Ethics is provided by NAYS in an attempt to persuade parents and coaches to unite to provide the most positive, safe, and fun youth sports program possible. The Coaches' Code of Ethics is shown in Chapter 3.

Most youth sports leagues have had to deal with the parental pressure issue in one way or another. Some have meetings of all parents; some leave it to the individual team managers and coaches to have meetings of their parents; some have volunteer parent liaison representatives, as in the case of the Soccer League of Montgomery County, Maryland, described above. For coauthor Ned McIntosh, in a Little League organization in which he coached, the parent problem became so acute that the league sent letters to all parents advising them that if their behavior did not improve, the league would ban parents from the Little League park. The letter stated that the league would allow parents to drop off their children at the entrance, give them two dollars to spend at the concession stand, and pick them up two hours later. Not surprisingly the parents' behavior in the stands improved. The league also reminded team managers and coaches that, in accordance with Little League rules, they had the responsibility of controlling the behavior of their fans, and that umpires had the authority to order the forfeit of a game if fan behavior could not be controlled.

We mentioned earlier in the book that parents' pressure to get their children involved in competitive sports at earlier and earlier ages has forced Little League baseball and youth soccer to start their programs at earlier ages. Just a few years ago the youngest age accepted was eight. Parents have various reasons for imposing pressure on youth sports organizations to start competitive sports training at earlier ages. In some cases the children are physically coordinated and/or emotionally ready. We recognize that chronological age and coordination age mesh at different ages for different children; and we wish parents would try to encourage their children to enter competitive sports at the proper age. Still many continue to force their children to compete too early—often to satisfy their own selfish desires. Many sports organizations have responded to the differences in physical coordination and emotional readiness by being flexible about the placement of a child, avoiding equal chronological age categories, in favor of equal coordination levels. They are doing it on a "readiness" basis, rather than a strict age basis. In soccer the level categories are defined as U8, U10, etc., the U meaning "under"; U8 is eight and under. That means that a child can play on a U8 team at any age under nine. League age is normally defined as the age of a player as of August 1 of the current year. Hence a gifted athlete of nine could be placed on a U12 team, while an uncoordinated nine-year-old would play on a U10 team.

Communication

The first meeting between parents and coaches should be held in the preseason. It should be preceded by a letter from the coach, such as the one shown in Exhibit 11.2, inviting parents to the meeting and explaining what they and their child should expect during the season.

Coauthor Jeff Thaler sends his personal letter to the parents of his team members, attached to a form letter from Ocean City Recreation and Parks to all parents (Exhibit 11.3), which also includes a copy of the Parent's Code of Ethics.

Dear Parents and Players:

Indoor soccer is here again, and I am pleased to welcome you to the Razorbacks Team's family of players, parents, and coaches. I will be depending on all of you to help us have a successful season.

Enclosed is a letter from the Town of Ocean City, whose Recreation and Parks Department is the sponsor of our recreational Soccer League. It contains important information for both players and their parents. With it is a copy of the Parent's Code of Ethics, which I would appreciate having a parent review, sign, and bring to our first meeting of players, parents, and coaches following our first practice, Wednesday evening, November 1, at 7:00 P.M. at the Rec Center, East Arena. The practice will be one hour, followed by a meeting in the community room. It should not last more than 30 minutes.

I am also enclosing the rosters of all of the teams in our division, so you can see on which teams your friends are playing, and who are your teammates. I will pass out our schedule at the meeting on November 1. Our first game is Saturday, November 4, at 10:00 A.M. Parents should have their children at games, dressed and ready to warm up at least 30 minutes before game time. (Shoes should be indoor sneakers; no cleats, please.)

If you have questions, now or at any time during the season, please feel free to call me at 555-3333.

Here's to a fun season!

Jeff Thaler, Razorbacks Head Coach

EXHIBIT 11.2   Coach's Letter

The first meeting with parents should serve the dual purpose of allowing the manager to recruit parent volunteers, as well as to review the team's plans and go over the coach's philosophy. Coaching a youth sports team is not a one-person responsibility. In both coauthors' experience, a minimum parent coaching team should include at least one assistant coach in addition to the head coach, a score and statistic keeper, and a team parent. We recommend that coaches explain that this is a team effort, not only for the players, but also for their parents. List the number of volunteer spots open, e.g., coaching, officiating, score and statistic keeping, phone committee, refreshments, transportation committee, etc. Ask each parent which of those volunteer assignments he or she would like to handle. (That's called giving them the choice of positives, and in a subtle way sets the philosophy that a parent has an *active* responsibility in helping to see that his or her child has a positive experience.)

You should explain to the parents that the coach is responsible for not only the behavior of the players, but also for the behavior of the team's supporters. Explain that the league philosophy recommends verbal support

Parents of Indoor Soccer,

Ocean City Recreation and Parks would like to welcome you and your children to the Recreational Soccer League. We are expecting lots of fun and great experiences this year. We have plenty of volunteers, staff, and building personnel to help you with any questions you may have. Please don't hesitate to ask. Our phone number at the Recreation and Parks complex is 410-555-4444. We are open Monday through Friday, 8:30 A.M. to 5:00 P.M.

Things to Remember

- Please be sure your child is on time for games. Arriving a few minutes early is helpful for the coaches.

- Dress your child appropriately. We are indoors, so slick-bottom shoes are a must, and shin guards are highly recommended for safety's sake.

- Children and siblings attending the games are not permitted to bring their own soccer balls. Please be sure to leave them at home. Our staff may hold them at the front desk if found during Recreational Play Day.

- We ask that all parents bringing children to watch the games keep a close eye on them. Climbing the walls is tempting but dangerous. **Please keep children off the Soccer Walls!**

- Liquids are good! We have a concession stand in our community room and several vending machines located through the buildings. Be sure your child drinks liquids.

Note: We understand the nature of "Game" play, but do not encourage competitive spirit during the Recreational Soccer League. We ask that all parents and spectators allow the Coaches (who have so generously volunteered) to do what is best for their teams. We have certified all of our coaches through the National Youth Sports Coaches Association, and assure you they are on the "everyone plays, everyone wins" philosophy with us at Ocean City Recreation and Parks. Please thank them for the great job they do and allow them to coach their team.

I have enclosed a Parent's Code of Ethics for you to read. Please read and understand that this is our philosophy here at Ocean City Recreation and Parks.

EXHIBIT 11.3 Form Letter from Sponsoring Organization

of the team and prohibits verbal criticism of the other team or the officials. Point out that an unruly spectator could be asked to leave the building, and refusing, could cause the forfeiture of the game by the very team he or she ostensibly supports.

Fortunately in most indoor soccer arenas the team benches are on one side of the rink, and the spectator stands on the other. In addition, the dasher boards and Plexiglas barriers keep spectators at a distance from the action, and tend to deaden the sound of an overly loud spectator—more so than in outdoor soccer or other outdoor sports. However, these factors didn't prevent the tragic murder of a coach at a youth hockey game.

"Kick It to the Middle, Joey!"

An article in the *Washington Post* gave an example of how a parent's out-of-control enthusiasm can be counterproductive to the coach's strategy. The parent was shouting to his child, "Kick it to the middle, Joey" at the same time the coach was calling, "Kick it to the side." In the combined 30 years of experience your coauthors have had coaching youth sports, we have encountered just about every negative parent situation in the book. For example, the parent who felt it was the responsibility of the coach to provide transportation to and from games for her child; the father who wanted to turn in his son's uniform, while the boy tearfully objected, because the coach had constructively counseled the boy on an obvious mistake; the parent who had refused to volunteer to help coach, yet loudly second-guessed the coaching strategy from the stands. None of these situations is ever positive or productive.

"But My Child Doesn't Play Enough"

A common complaint from a subjective parent centers on playing time and/or why his or her child wasn't in the starting lineup. One father claimed he had a stopwatch to keep track of the time his child played, and objected bitterly when it appeared the child had played fewer minutes than the other players. As mentioned earlier, the fast pace of the nonstop action in indoor arena soccer minimizes this complaint, as frequent substituting is both necessary and a sound strategy; why wouldn't you want to have fresh, rested players relieving their tired teammates? But the fact remains that many parents cannot be objective about their own child. If a child tearfully complains to an overprotective parent that either the coach or the referee was unfair, that parent may overreact. The only answer a coach can give to the parent who complains that his or her child wasn't in the starting lineup is that the starting lineup isn't all that significant, since all children will ride the bench during the course of the game. The coach may mention that he or she will make every effort to give all players equal playing time.

A second parent meeting, midseason, is recommended. By that time, the coaches and parents will have had some experience under their collective belts, and there undoubtedly will be questions. Of course, in the preseason meeting you should encourage the parents to communicate with you at any time, either in person after games or via phone. You should encourage feedback from them about whether their child is having fun, and if not, what seems to be the problem. Coauthor Jeff Thaler uses a good technique in dealing with a critical parent. He invites him or her to sit on the bench at a game, as assistant coach for the day. When parents get an up-close view of what goes on, it helps them empathize better with the coach.

By the season's end, the coach and the parents are likely to be old friends, all reading from the same page. At that point, a celebration meeting is in order. Hopefully a winning season will be the reason for the celebration. It is always more fun to win, and a winning season (more wins than losses) is what we virtually guarantee you if you follow the guidelines presented in the next chapter.

CHAPTER 12

Winning

There is an old adage that goes something like this: "I've been poor and I've been rich, and rich is better." To translate that to sports and fun, if your team has lost and your team has won then you all know that winning is better—and more fun! Simply put, your players will have more fun when your team wins, and so will you. Some parents and coaches aren't satisfied unless their team wins *every* game, or at least the league championship. Unfortunately, that attitude toward winning creates the kind of pressure that takes the fun out of playing. We encourage our players to "play hard to win," which is not the same as the oft-quoted philosophy in professional sports that "winning is everything." Trying to win is not inconsistent with the philosophy we have espoused throughout this book of "Keep it simple; make it fun." We are certainly not advocating that you make winning your top priority. We will give you a tested formula in this chapter of how you can have a winning season—a season in which your team will win more games than it loses—if you are willing to dedicate the time and commitment. It is a simple formula based on time spent. The more time you and your team spend practicing, the more games you will win. If you follow our formula, you and your players will have *more* fun, partly because you will win more games. Consistently losing is demoralizing to spirit and morale, cuts down on player attendance, and is no fun.

We your coauthors have outstanding records for managing winning teams during our combined experience of more than 30 years as volunteer coaches of youth sports, following the philosophy of "Keep it simple and make it fun." It is our tested formula of success in maximizing fun and winning that we are sharing with you. Our definition of a winning team is simply a team that wins more games than it loses. After all, winning can't be fully appreciated unless you can compare it to the humbling experience of losing. We can't guarantee you an undefeated season, or a championship team, but we can virtually guarantee you a winning season. But that means following each of the elements of coaching that we have outlined in this book—plus the final piece of the puzzle: practice, practice, and practice.

We mean practice *every* day. Soccer is a game of skills that can be perfected simply through repetitive drills, practice after practice after practice. Take a young player who can't dribble, and run him through the copycat dribble drill 20 times, following your best dribbler, and he will learn to dribble. Have her bounce the ball off the back wall 50 times and follow the ricochet with a shot on goal, and she will become an accomplished shooter.

"But I can't take the time to practice my team every day," you say. We didn't say *you* have to be there every day (although it would be nice if you could). Your players will be there, you can bet on that. We encourage you to bring one or more assistant coaches on board. Surely this will help you to arrange for at least one coach to be there every day.

"But the parents will object," you say. "They will refuse to bring and pick up their youngster *every* day." Fast-forward to the day their youngster makes the All-Star team, and the coach announces daily practice for the next three weeks while the team is groomed for the first All-Star tournament game. Will they refuse to bring and pick up their youngster every day for *that*? You know they won't. What about when their youngster makes the high school soccer team? Don't they practice every day?

Now fast-forward to the present. Why is it any less important for a youngster to practice *every day* now with his or her soccer team to learn how to become a better ball player, coached by someone who believes in making it simple and keeping it fun? We think the child will persuade his or her parent that it *is* important to be at practice *every* day.

"But what if I can't get a practice field every day?" you say. Depending on your area, this could present a problem. One that requires a little ingenuity. In this book we separate the practice skills into two chapters. Chapter 7 contains the off-the-wall skills and drills—those that *do* require an arena for practice. However, Chapter 6 includes the skills, drills, and games that can be practiced anywhere there is a flat surface, for example, a field or unused parking lot in good weather or a school or church gym in bad weather. Encourage parents to provide a soccer ball for each player, so kids can practice on their own, or with a parent or sibling. On the days when it is impossible to have team practice, urge your players to spend the same amount of time practicing at home. Many successful soccer players at the college and professional level will recount the hours they spent bouncing a soccer ball against steps or a wall at home as a youngster. Challenge your players to stay focused on becoming better soccer players by not missing a day of practice—either team or individual. Give your players practice cards, and ask them to have a parent sign off on the days and times they practice on their own.

As we mentioned in Chapter 8, we encourage you to have skull sessions with your players to help them understand the rationale of the drills and game strategies. You can mark off the outline of the soccer playing area, showing the various lines and circles, on a blank sheet of paper, and use red and black checker pieces to indicate the positions of the players in various game situations. Scheduling one skull session a week at your home will provide variety in your practice routine and will pay off when you see your players put their heads into the game as well as their physical skills. Create game situations, both offensive and defensive, and get them to recommend the proper strategy. Recap actual recent game situations and get them to think through what went well and what could have been improved. Make up quizzes to measure what the players have learned. Give inexpensive motivational things to those who achieve the best scores. The test results will tell you two important things: what they haven't learned, so you can spend more time on those things; and who your most savvy players are. You may be surprised to find the best students of the game are not the most advanced physically. If you have a parent with a

The coach conducts a skull session using an erasable clipboard to diagram a play or drill.

camcorder, ask him or her to tape some of your games. Then play the tapes at skull practice.

There are some things you can do as the coach of an indoor soccer team to help your team have a winning season—before the season begins. Following are some of the more important ones.

Scout for Players

Do you know any professional NFL or NBA team that doesn't scout for talent among the college teams in their respective sports? To quote Yogi Berra, "You can't win ball games without players." Most soccer leagues have tryouts, followed by a draft of players, to determine which players play on what teams. Check with your league to find out their rules for assigning players to teams. Some leagues will protect previous players on a team from tryouts and draft, which means they'll allow you to keep age-appropriate, experienced players as a nucleus around which to build the current year's team. In such a case, you will need only to fill vacancies from the tryouts/draft. Other leagues will not protect players, except for children of coaches, and you will have to start with a virtually clean slate for this year's roster. In either case, you need to prepare for the tryouts and draft by finding out who are the potentially good athletes in your team's age class. Analyze what you need to build a well-balanced team. It should be balanced from the standpoints of both ability and age.

Normally age levels are established on even years—U8, U10, U12, and so forth—with the child's age on August 1 determining which age bracket a child will play in. (Check this date with your league.) Practically speaking, it means players will play for two years in each successive bracket. If your league allows retention of age-appropriate players, then you will want a balance between the two ages so that you will have some experienced players returning next year. In any event, the tryouts and draft are important. You can be sure the coaches of all professional teams have done their homework in scouting the best prospects in the draft, and so should you.

Normally the coach's son or daughter will automatically be assigned to the coach's team. But don't wait for tryouts to do your scouting. Most gifted athletes will be good at whatever sport they try, so you would be well advised to find out who the best baseball players are from this spring's Little League season and who the best athletes are in intramural school sports. Your children can help target good players for you. Talk to school coaches and the Little League coaches to get the names of the All-Stars. If you didn't coach soccer the previous year, talk to some coaches who did, particularly coaches who graduated players from their team's lower age-group up to your team's. If you are inheriting a team with players who will automatically stay with your team, have a meeting with them to brainstorm who the best available soccer players are. Ask them and your children if any new kids have moved into the area, and try to find out if they have any previous soccer experience. You will then be able to go to the tryouts with a list of prospects, and then see if they are as good as advertised.

Tryouts

A good league generally has more than one tryout day so that a player who has other commitments on the first day will have an opportunity to try out on an alternate day. Beware of overzealous coaches who may advise a good player to register but skip tryouts. That coach would then have an advantage over other coaches in the draft who would not have seen the good player in a tryout and who would be forced to draft him blind. Encourage your league to have a rule that *all* registered players *must* participate in the tryouts to be eligible for the draft. If your league has that rule, then you have the same opportunity as every other coach to do your homework before the tryouts and the draft.

At tryouts, in addition to the skills of dribbling, passing, and controlling, you are looking for players with speed and size, probably in that order of priority. For all of the reasons we have covered in this book so far, a good, fast player is your best prospect for indoor soccer. If the tryouts include timed foot races, check out the fastest prospects from those results. If a player is big, he or she has certain obvious advantages on defense and one-on-one encounters. If he or she is both big and fast you have a double advantage. Look also for left-footed players. They will have certain advantages in encounters with right-footed players, and will give your offense balance if you can put a left-footed player on the left wing. Look for the player who can sniff the goal—in other words, someone who has an aggressive feel for scoring.

Girls are often chosen last in the draft, but be aware that girls often mature sooner in the important area of coordination, so look for quick, well-coordinated girls. To evaluate a prospect's ability at ball control in the tryouts, ball juggling will probably be the exercise they ask each player to do. Watch this tryout skill carefully, because a player who is adept at juggling the ball from foot to chest to knee, while balancing on one leg, like a flamingo will be a good prospect.

When you see a big left-footed kicker in tryouts, put him or her down as a good prospect in the draft.

This prospect shows promise as he balances on one leg while juggling the ball with his other.

"Sniff Out the Goal" Aptitude

Another good aptitude to look for in tryouts is sense of the field—players who know where they are and where they need to be. Many youth soccer players can kick the ball hard, which is good, but having the sense of scoring—"sniffing out the goal"—is a special soccer trait that is almost instinctive in a gifted soccer player. In other sports it is often called the killer instinct—aggressive skill on offense.

Children of the Coach

One of your coauthors, Ned McIntosh, had an experience in drafting that bears mentioning, as it conceivably could happen to you. It was in a league that allowed teams to retain players from the previous year. He drafted a gifted nine-year-old player for a U12 team, and coached him for two years. The following year, the boy's father became a coach and claimed his son for his team, which he had every right to do. But that meant Ned was losing a star player he had groomed for a key role. The league stepped in and recommended the two coaches handle it the same way the pros do, with either a trade or a draft pick as compensation. They did, and everybody was happy.

Recruit Coaches to Help You

Generally the parent of a gifted athlete will be interested in his or her child's team, so you could get an extra bonus by recruiting the child *and* his or her parent to help you. As mentioned earlier, you will need all the help you can get, particularly if you commit to daily practices. Also check to see if your league has a sibling rule, a provision stipulating that siblings will play on the same team for the convenience of the parents in bringing their children to practice.

Keep Statistics

Speed is important in indoor soccer, and you will want to know who are your fastest players. The best way to find out is to get a stopwatch and conduct foot races periodically. During games you should have an assistant coach keeping statistics for you. You will want to keep track of goals scored, goals attempted, assists, and saves. Don't rely on your memory. This cumulative data will help you determine what combination of players will comprise your strongest line.

Motivation

Coaching kids can be frustrating sometimes, but most of the time it's rewarding. Young players are so trusting and impressionable that it places a heavy responsibility on the adult coach who must justify their trust and impress them in a positive way.

Keeping things in perspective—remembering to keep it simple and make it fun—is the coach's biggest challenge. It is sometimes difficult to empathize with the player who blew it in a close game. But empathize we must! A pat on the back or reassuring word, instead of a dirty look or a negative comment, can go a long way toward defusing the pressure and sense of failure the youngster is feeling. Getting the coach's approval is important to a kid, and a sensitive coach will soon recognize what a great motivator encouragement is.

A coach can motivate his or her team during the pregame meeting and postgame meeting. We recommend these meetings be held away from parents, as some parents can be a distraction. Sometimes little inexpensive motivators can be worth their weight in gold. Even a piece of bubble gum can seem like a great reward if it's given at the right moment. We recommend you keep a notebook of personal accomplishments players make during the game, so that in your post-game meeting you can recall them and praise the players who did something special. Forgetting to praise one, when you have praised others, can have a negative effect. Be sure to outline what a player needs to do to get special recognition; for example, you might reward players for their first goal or first assist, as well as significant accomplishments, such as shutout for a goalie. You might even name an MVP for each game. Have inexpensive rewards to give out, such as wrist bands or headbands in the team's colors, hacky sacks, miniature soccer balls, and water bottles. A miniature soccer ball could be the MVP award; you can write on it with a marker the name of the player, date, score, and opponent. The best inexpensive motivators coauthor Ned McIntosh discovered were shoulder stars, which are similar to the stars that some football

This goalie pitched a shutout, so he gets the MVP award, a water bottle in the team's colors.

Two players show off their shoulder stars, after-game awards they received for doing something that was exceptional for their age and ability.

teams put on their players' helmets. Ned gave out felt stars that the players' parents could sew on the shoulders of their jerseys, coordinating the color with the shirt. He kept a supply on hand in individual envelopes and gave them out in the team meeting at the end of each game. They were geared to the age and ability of the players, so something that might be routine for an all-star player was often exceptional for a rookie. You can tell how significant the stars are to your players when you begin to notice how quickly they have them sewn onto their jerseys.

Don't praise only the players who scored goals, but also those who delivered the passes that made the goal possible. Also be sure to compliment players on great defensive plays or saves. Spread praise evenly. After all without the defense many more goals would have been scored against you. If a win was a team effort, every member of the team could get a star. Always try to end your postgame meeting on a high, whether you won or lost. Stars can be given for individual effort, even after a loss. Give the players something positive to look forward to. When the game ends and the two teams line up, have your MVP—whether it's the player who scored the winning goal or the goalie that saved the game—lead the team as they shake hands with members of the opposing team.

The game's MVP, holding his award, leads the team in the traditional postgame handshaking ceremony.

As a coach, you will have a winning season if you put in the necessary time and if your players practice, practice, practice. And you personally will be a winner in the eyes of your kids if they remember you as a coach who always recognized their triumphs and empathized with their defeats. Long after they have forgotten the scores of the games, they will still remember the coach who cared about them.

Index

Page numbers in italics indicate pages with photos or illustrations.

Winning season, 37, 106, 107, 110, 115

Winterfest Soccer Camp, 33–35

Women's soccer, 1, 2

World Cup, 1–2, 14, 15, 37, 67

Yellow card offenses, 92, 93

YMCA, 3, 7, 9, 28

Youth Sports Institute, 100

Youth Sports Journal, 17

Zirkes, Arnold, 23